MORE HIGH SCHOOL Talksheets

50 ALL NEW creative discussions
for high school youth groups

David Lynn

Youth
Specialties

ZondervanPublishingHouse

A Division of HarperCollins *Publishers*

ZONDERVAN/YOUTH SPECIALTIES BOOKS

Professional Resources

Called to Care
Developing Student Leaders
Feeding Your Forgotten Soul
Growing Up in America
High School Ministry
How to Recruit and Train Volunteer Youth Workers
    (Previously released as Unsung Heroes)
Junior High Ministry (Revised Edition)
The Ministry of Nurture
Organizing Your Youth Ministry
Peer Counseling in Youth Groups
The Youth Minister's Survival Guide
Youth Ministry Nuts and Bolts

Discussion Starter Resources

Get 'Em Talking
Hot Talks
More High School TalkSheets
Option Plays

Special Needs and Issues

The Complete Student Missions Handbook
Divorce Recovery for Teenagers
Ideas for Social Action
Intensive Care: Helping Teenagers in Crisis
Up Close and Personal: How to Build Community
    in Your Youth Group

Youth Ministry Programming

Adventure Games
Creative Programming Ideas for Junior High Ministry
Creative Socials and Special Events
Good Clean Fun
Good Clean Fun, Volume 2
Great Games for City Kids
Great Ideas for Small Youth Groups
Greatest Skits on Earth
Greatest Skits on Earth, Volume 2
Holiday Ideas for Youth Groups (Revised Edition)
Junior High Game Nights
More Junior High Game Nights
On-Site: 40 On-Location Youth Programs
Play It! Great Games for Groups
Super Sketches for Youth Ministry
Teaching the Bible Creatively
The Youth Specialties Handbook for Great
    Camps and Retreats

4th-6th Grade Ministry

How to Survive Middle School
Incredible Stories

Clip Art

ArtSource™ Volume 1—Fantastic Activities
ArtSource™ Volume 2—Borders, Symbols, Holidays,
    and Attention Getters
ArtSource™ Volume 3—Sports
ArtSource™ Volume 4—Phrases and Verses
ArtSource™ Volume 5—Amazing Oddities and
    Appalling Images
ArtSource™ Volume 6—Spiritual Topics
Youth Specialties Clip Art Book
Youth Specialties Clip Art Book, Volume 2

Video

Next Time I Fall In Love Video Curriculum
Understanding Your Teenager Video Curriculum
Video Spots for Junior High Game Nights

OTHER BOOKS BY DAVID LYNN

Amazing Tension Getters—with Mike Yaconelli
    (Zondervan/Youth Specialties)
Attention Grabbers for 4th-6th Graders (Zondervan/
    Youth Specialties)
Great Games for 4th-6th Graders (Zondervan/Youth
    Specialties)
Grow For It Journal—with Mike Yaconelli
    (Zondervan/Youth Specialties)
High School TalkSheets (Zondervan/Youth Special-
    ties)
Junior High TalkSheets (Zondervan/Youth Special-
    ties)
More Attention Grabbers for 4th-6th Graders
    (Zondervan/Youth Specialties)
More Great Games for 4th-6th Graders (Zondervan/
    Youth Specialties)
More Junior High TalkSheets (Zondervan/Youth Spe-
    cialties)
More Quick and Easy Activities for 4th-6th Graders
    (Zondervan/Youth Specialties)
More Zingers: 25 Real-Life Character Builders
    (Zondervan)
Parent Ministry TalkSheets (Zondervan/Youth
    Specialties)
Quick and Easy Activities for 4th-6th Graders
    (Zondervan/Youth Specialties)
Rock Talk (Zondervan/Youth Specialties)
Teaching the Truth About Sex—with Mike Yaconelli
    (Zondervan/Youth Specialties)
Tension Getters—with Mike Yaconelli (Zondervan/
    Youth Specialties)
Tension Getters Two—with Mike Yaconelli
    (Zondervan/Youth Specialties)
Twisters: Questions You Never Thought to Ask!
    (Zondervan)
Zingers: 25 Real-Life Character Builders (Zondervan)

More High School TalkSheets

Copyright © 1992 by Youth Specialties, Inc.

Youth Specialties Books, 1224 Greenfield Drive, El Cajon, California 92021,
are published by Zondervan Publishing House, 5300 Patterson, S.E., Grand Rapids, Michigan 49530

ISBN 0-310-57491-9

Edited by Lory Floyd and Elizabeth Abbott
Art Director Mark Rayburn
Typography and design by The Church Art Works
Cover illustration by John Bolesky
Illustrations by Bruce Day

Printed in the United States of America

98 99 00 01 02 ML 16 15 14 13 12

Table of Contents

Table of Contents (continued)

HOW TO USE TALKSHEETS

You have in your possession a very valuable book. It contains 50 instant youth group discussions for high school youth groups. Inside, you will find reproducible "TalkSheets" covering a wide variety of "hot topics," plus simple step-by-step instructions on how to use them. All you need for 50 thought-provoking meetings is this book and access to a copy machine.

TalkSheets are versatile and easy to use. They can be used in a group meeting, a Sunday school class, or during a Bible study group. They can be used either in small or large groups of people. The discussions they instigate can be as brief as 20 minutes or as long as interest remains and time allows. You can build an entire youth group meeting around a single TalkSheet or you can use TalkSheets to supplement other materials and resources you might be using. The possibilities are endless.

TalkSheets are much more than just another type of curriculum or workbook. They invite excitement and involvement in discussing important issues and growth in faith. Talksheets deal with key topics that young people want to talk about. With interesting activities, challenging questions, and eye-catching graphics, TalkSheets will capture the attention of your audience and will help them think and learn. The more you use TalkSheets, the more your young people will look forward to them.

TALKSHEETS ARE DISCUSSION STARTERS

Although TalkSheets can be used as curricula for your program, they are primarily designed to be used as discussion starters. Everyone knows the value of a good discussion in which young people are interacting with each other. When they are talking about a given subject, they are most likely thinking seriously about it and trying to understand it better. They are formulating and defending their points of view and making decisions and choices. Discussion helps truth rise to the surface thereby making it easier for young people to discover it for themselves. There is no better way to encourage learning than through discussion.

A common fear among youth group leaders reticent about leading a group of teenagers in discussion is "What if the kids in my group just sit there and refuse to participate?" It is because of this fear that many choose to show a movie or give a prepared lecture.

Usually the reason young people fail to take part in a discussion is simple: they haven't had the time or the opportunity to organize their thoughts. Most high school students haven't yet developed the ability to "think on their feet"—to be able to present their ideas spontaneously and with confidence. They are afraid to speak for fear they might sound stupid.

TalkSheets remove this fear. They offer a chance to interact with the subject matter in an interesting, challenging, and nonthreatening way, *before* the actual discussion begins. Not only does this give them time to organize their thoughts and to write them down, but it also helps remove any anxiety they might feel. Most will actually look forward to sharing their answers and hearing others' responses to the same questions. They will be ready for a lively discussion.

A STEP-BY-STEP USER'S GUIDE

TalkSheets are very easy to use, but do require some preparation on your part. Follow these simple instructions and your TalkSheet discussion will be successful.

1 **Choose the right TalkSheet for your group.** Each TalkSheet deals with a different topic. The one you choose will have a lot to do with the needs and the maturity level of your group. It is not necessary (or recommended) to use the TalkSheets in the order in which they appear in this book.

2 **Try it yourself.** Once you have chosen a specific TalkSheet, answer the questions and do the activities yourself. Imagine your students participating. This "role playing" will give you firsthand knowledge of what you will be requiring of your young people. As you fill out the TalkSheet, think of additional questions, activities, and Scriptures.

3 Read the Leader's Instructions on the back of each TalkSheet. Numerous tips and ideas for getting the most out of your discussion are contained in the Leader's Instructions. Add your own thoughts and ideas. Fill in the date and the name of the group at the top of each leader's page.

4 Remove the TalkSheet from the book. The pages are perforated along the left margins for easy removal. The information is easier to copy when removed. Before making copies, you might wish to "white out" (with liquid paper) the page number.

5 Make enough copies for everyone. Each student will need his or her own copy. This book makes the assumption that you have access to a copy machine. Only the student's side of the TalkSheet needs to be copied. The leader's material on the other side is just for you, the leader.

Keep in mind that you are able to make copies for your group because we have given you permission to do so. (U.S. copyright laws still mandate that you request permission from a publisher before making copies of any other published material. It is illegal not to do so.) Permission is given for you to make copies of this material for *your own group only*, not for every youth group in your state. Thank you for your cooperation.

6 Introduce the topic. In most cases, it is important to introduce or "set up" the topic before you pass out the TalkSheets to your group. Any method will do as long as it is short and to the point. Be careful not to "over introduce" the subject. Don't use an introduction that is too "preachy" or that resolves the issue before you get started. You want only to stimulate interest and instigate discussion. That is the primary purpose of the introduction. The simplest way to introduce the topic is verbally. You can tell a story, share an experience, or describe a conflict having to do with the subject. You might ask a simple question, such as "What is the first thing you think of when you hear the word _____?" (whatever the topic is). After some have volunteered a few answers, you could reply, "It sounds like we all have different ideas on the subject; let's investigate it a bit further . . ." or something similar. Then you can distribute the TalkSheets, making certain everyone has a pen or a pencil, and you're on your way.

Here are some ways of introducing any of the topics in this book, all of which, of course, should be pertinent:

    a. Show a short film or video.
    b. Read an interesting passage from a book or a magazine article.
    c. Play a popular song dealing with the theme.
    d. Present a short skit or dramatic reading.
    e. Play a simulation game or role-play.
    f. Present some current statistics, survey results, or read a recent newspaper article.
    g. Use an "ice breaker," such as a humorous game.
    h. Use posters, slides, or any other audiovisual aids available to help concentrate focus.

There are, of course, many other possibilities. The introduction of the topic is left to your discretion and good judgment. You are limited only by your own creativity. Suggestions are offered with each TalkSheet, but they are not mandatory for success. Remember that the introduction is an integral part of each session. It helps set the tone and will influence the kinds of responses you receive. Don't "load" the introduction to the point that the "answer" is revealed and the students feel hesitant about sharing their own opinions.

7 Give students time to work on their TalkSheets. After your introduction of the topic, pass out a copy of the TalkSheet to each member of the group. They should also have a copy of the Bible, as well as writing implements. There are usually five to six activities on each TalkSheet. If time is limited, direct your students' interest to the specific part of the TalkSheet in which you wish them to participate.

Decide whether or not they should complete the TalkSheet on an individual basis or in groups. Encourage your group to consider what the Bible has to say as they complete their TalkSheets.

Announce a time limit for their written work, then make them aware when one or two minutes remain. They may need more time, or less. Use your own judgment, depending upon your observations of the majority of the group. The discussion is now ready to begin.

8 Lead the discussion. In order for the TalkSheets to be used effectively, all members of your group need to be encouraged to participate. You must foster a climate that is conducive to discussion by communicating that each person's opinion is worthwhile and each has a responsibility to contribute to the rest of the group. A variety of opinions is necessary for these TalkSheets to have meaning.

If your group is large, you may want to divide it into smaller ones of six to 12 each. One person in each smaller group should be appointed facilitator to keep the discussion alive. The facilitator can be either an adult or another young person. Advise the leaders not to try and dominate the group, but to be on the same level with each member. If the group looks to the facilitator for the "answer," have the leader direct the questions or responses back to the group. Once the smaller groups have completed their discussions, have them reassemble into one large group, move through the items again, and ask the different sections to summarize what they learned from each activity.

It is not necessary to divide up into groups every time TalkSheets are used. Variations provide more interest. You may prefer, at times, to have smaller groups of the same sex.

The discussion should center around the questions and answers on the TalkSheet. Go through them one at a time, asking volunteers to share how they responded to each item. Have them compare their answers and brainstorm new ones in addition to those they wrote down. Allow those who don't feel comfortable revealing their answers to remain silent.

Don't feel pressured to spend time on each activity. If time does not permit a discussion of every item, feel free to focus attention only on those provoking the higher interest.

Move with your own creative instinct. If you discover a better or different way to use the activity, do so. Don't feel restricted by the leader's instructions on the back of the TalkSheet. Use Scriptures not found on the TalkSheet. Add your own items. TalkSheets were designed for you to be able to add your own thoughts and ideas.

If the group begins to digress about an issue that has nothing to do with the main topic, guide it back on track. If, however, there is a high degree of interest in this "side issue," you may wish to allow the "extra" discussion. It may meet a need of many in the group and, therefore, be worth pursuing. More information on leading discussions is found in the next section.

Wrap up the discussion. This is your chance to challenge the group. When considering your closing remarks, ask yourself the following question: What do I want the group to remember from this experience? If you can answer in two or three sentences, then you have your closing remarks. It is important to bring some sort of closure to the session without negating the thoughts and opinions expressed by the group. A good wrap-up should affirm the group and offer a summary that helps tie the discussion together. Your students should be left with the desire to discuss the issue further, among themselves or with a leader. Tell your group members you are available to discuss the issue privately after the meeting. In some cases, a wrap-up may be unnecessary; just leave the issue hanging and bring it up again at a later date. This allows your students to wrestle with the issue on their own. Later, resolutions can evolve.

Follow up with an additional activity. The leader's instructions on the back of the TalkSheet provide you with ideas for additional activities. They are optional but highly recommended. Their purpose is to afford an opportunity to reflect upon, evaluate, review, and integrate what has been learned. Most of your TalkSheet discussions will generate a desire to discuss the subject matter again, which leads to better assimilation and more learning.

Assign the activity and follow up on the assignment with a short, debriefing talk at the next group meeting. Appropriate questions about the activity could include the following:

    a. What happened when you did this activity? Was it helpful or a waste of time?
    b. How did you feel while you were doing the activity?
    c. Did the activity change your mind or affect you in some way?
    d. In one sentence, tell what you learned from this activity.

HOW TO LEAD A TALKSHEET DISCUSSION

The young people of today are growing up in a world of moral confusion. The problem facing youth workers in the church is not so much how to teach the church's doctrines but how to help teens make the right choices when faced with so many options. The church's response to this problem has traditionally been to indoctrinate—to preach and yell its point of view louder than the rest of the world. This kind of approach does not work in today's world. Teenagers are hearing a variety of voices and messages, most of which are louder than those they hear from the church.

A TalkSheet discussion is effective for just this reason. While discussing the questions and activities on the TalkSheet, your students will be encouraged to think carefully about issues, to compare their beliefs and values with others, and to learn to make discerning choices. TalkSheets will challenge your group to evaluate, defend, explain, and rework their ideas in an atmosphere of acceptance, support, and growth.

CHARACTERISTICS OF A TALKSHEET DISCUSSION

Remember, successful discussions—those that produce learning and growth—rarely happen by accident. They require careful preparation and sensitive leadership. Don't be concerned if you feel you lack experience at this time or don't have the time to spend for a lengthy preparation. The more TalkSheet discussions you lead, the easier they will become and the more skilled you will be. It will help if you read the material on the next few pages and try to incorporate these ideas into your discussions.

The following suggestions will assist you in reaching a maximum level of success:

Create a climate of acceptance. Most teenagers are afraid to express their opinions because they are fearful of what others might think. Peer approval is paramount with teenagers. They are fearful of being ridiculed or thought of as being "dumb." They need to feel secure before they share their feelings and beliefs. They also need to know they can share what they are thinking, no matter how unpopular or "wild" their ideas might be. If any of your students are subjected to put-downs, criticism, laughter, or judgmental comments, especially if what they say is opposed to the teachings of the Bible or the church or their leader, an effective discussion will not be forthcoming.

For this reason, each TalkSheet begins with a question or activity less threatening and more fun than some that follow. The first question helps the individuals to become more comfortable with each other and with the prospect of sharing their ideas more openly.

When asking a question, even one that is printed on the TalkSheets, phrase it to evoke *opinions*, not *answers*. In other words, instead of saying, "What should Jessica have done in that situation?" change it to "What do you *think* Jessica should have done?" The addition of the three words "do you think" makes the question a matter of opinion, rather than a matter of knowing the right answer. When young people realize their opinions are all that are necessary, they will be more apt to feel comfortable and confident.

Affirm all legitimate expressions of opinion from your group members. Let each person know her or his comments and contributions are appreciated and important. This is especially true for those who rarely participate. When they do, make a point of thanking them. This will encourage them and make them feel appreciated.

Keep in mind affirmation does not necessarily mean approval. Affirm even those comments that seem like heresy to you. By doing so, you let the group know all have the right to express their ideas, no matter what they are. If someone does express an opinion that you believe is way off base and needs to be corrected, make a mental note of the comment and present an alternative point of view in your concluding remarks, in a positive way. Don't attack or condemn the person who made the comment.

Discourage the group from thinking of you as the "authority" on the subject. Sometimes young people will think you have the "right answer" to every question and they will watch for your reaction, even when they are answering someone else's questions. If you find the group's responses are slanted toward your approval, redirect them to the whole group. For example, you could say, "Talk to the group, not to me" or "Tell everyone, not just me."

It is important for you to try to let them see you as a "facilitator"—another member of the group who is helping make the discussion happen. You are not sitting in judgment of their responses, nor do you have the right answer to every problem.

Remember, with teenagers, your opinions will carry more weight the less of an authority figure you appear to be. If you are regarded as an affirming friend, they will pay much more attention to what you have to say.

Actively listen to each person. God gave you one mouth and two ears. Good discussion leaders know how to listen. Your job is not to monopolize the discussion or to contribute the wisest words on each issue. Keep your mouth shut except when you are encouraging others to talk. You are a *facilitator*. You can express your opinions during your concluding remarks.

Do not force anyone to talk. Invite people to speak out, but don't attempt to force them to do so. Each member needs to have the right to "pass."

Do not take sides during the discussion. You will have disagreements in your group from time to time and students who will take opposing viewpoints. Don't make the mistake of siding with one group or the other. Encourage both sides to think though their positions and to defend their points of view. You might ask probing questions of both, to encourage deeper introspection of all ideas. If everyone seems to agree on a question, or if they seem fearful of expressing a controversial opinion, it might be beneficial for you to play devil's advocate with some thought-provoking comments. This will force them to think. Do not give them the impression that the "other" point of view is necessarily your own. Remain neutral.

Do not allow one person—including yourself—to monopolize the discussion. Almost every group has that one person who likes to talk and is perfectly willing to express her or his opinion on every question. Try to encourage everyone to participate.

Arrange seating to encourage discussion. "Theater style" seating—in rows—is not conducive to conversation. If you will be using chairs at all, arrange them in a circular or semi-circular pattern. Occasionally, smaller groups of four to six are less threatening to teenagers, especially if there is a variety of maturity levels in the group. If you have both junior high level and senior high level in the same group, it might be preferable to segregate them accordingly.

Allow for humor when appropriate. Do not take the discussions so seriously as to prohibit humor. Most TalkSheets include questions that will generate laughter as well as some intense dialogue.

Don't be afraid of silence. Many discussion leaders are intimidated by silence in a group. Their first reaction is to fill the silence with a question or a comment. The following suggestions may help you handle silence more effectively:

a. Learn to feel comfortable with silence. Wait it out for 30 seconds. Give someone a reasonable time to volunteer a response. If you feel it is appropriate, invite a specific person to talk. Sometimes a gentle nudge is all that is necessary.

b. Discuss the silence with the group. Ask them what the silence really means. Perhaps they are confused or embarrassed and don't feel free to share their thoughts.

c. Answer the silence with questions or comments about it, such as "It's a difficult issue to consider, isn't it?" or "It's scary to be the first to talk." This might break the ice.

d. Ask a different question that might be easier to handle or that might clarify the one that has been proposed. But don't do this too quickly. Wait a short while, first.

Try to keep the discussion under control. Frequently a discussion can become sidetracked onto a subject you may not consider desirable. If someone brings up a side issue that generates a lot of interest, you will need to decide whether or not to pursue that issue and see where it leads or redirect the conversation back to the original subject. Sometimes it's a good idea to digress—especially if the interest is high and the issue worth discussing. In most cases, however, it is advisable to say something like "Let's come back to that subject a little later, if we have the time. Right now, let's finish our discussion on . . .".

Be creative and flexible. Do not feel compelled to ask every question on the TalkSheet, one by one, in order. If you wish, ask only a couple of them, or add a few of your own. The leader's guide may give you some ideas, but think of your own as well. Each question or activity may lead to several others along the same lines that you can ask during the discussion.

Be an "askable" discussion leader. Make certain your young people understand they can talk to you about anything and find concern and support, even after the TalkSheet discussion has been completed.

Know what your goals are. A TalkSheet discussion should be more than just a "bull session." TalkSheets are designed to move the conversation toward a goal, but you will need to identify that goal in advance. What would you like the young people to learn? What truth would you like them to discover? What is the goal of the session? If you don't know where you are going, it is doubtful you will arrive.

GROUND RULES FOR AN EFFECTIVE TALKSHEET DISCUSSION

A few ground rules will be helpful before beginning your TalkSheet discussions. Rules should be kept to a minimum, but most of the time young people will respond in a positive manner if they know in advance what is expected of them. The following are suggestions for you to consider using:

"What is said in this room stays in this room."

Confidentiality is vitally important to a healthy discussion. The only time it should be broken is if a group member reveals he or she is going to do harm to himself or herself or another person.

"No put-downs."

Mutual respect is important. If someone disagrees with another's comment, he or she should raise his or her hand and express an opinion on the *comment*, but not of the person who made it. It is permissible to attack ideas, but not each other.

"There is no such thing as a dumb question."

Your youths and adult leaders must feel free to ask questions at any time. Asking questions is the best way to learn.

"No one is forced to talk."

Let all members know they have the right to remain silent about any question.

"Only one person talks at a time."

This is a good way to teach young people mutual respect. Each person's opinion is worthwhile and deserves to be heard.

If members of the group violate these rules during the discussion or engage in disruptive or negative behavior, it would be wise to stop and deal with the problem before continuing.

USING THE BIBLE WITH THE TALKSHEETS

Adults often begin discussions with young people assuming they believe the Bible has authority over their lives. Adults either begin their discussions with Scripture or quickly support their contentions with Bible verses. Young people of today often consider their life situations first, then decide if the Bible fits. TalkSheets have been designed to deliberately begin your discussion with the realities of the adolescent world and then move toward Scripture. This gives you the opportunity to show them the Bible can be their guide and God does have something to say that is applicable to their age level and their interests.

The last activity on each TalkSheet involves Scripture. These Bible references were selected for their relevance to each issue and for their potential to generate healthy discussion. They are not to be considered exhaustive. It was assumed you will add whatever Scriptures you believe are equally pertinent. The passages listed are only the tip of the iceberg, inviting you to "search the Scriptures" for more.

Once the Scriptures have been read aloud, ask your group to develop a biblical principle that can guide their lives. For example, after reading the passages on the topic of Christian service ("Going Crazy with God"), the group may summarize by saying, "The Gospel is more than simply telling others about Christ's love and forgiveness. The Lord also wants us to serve him by serving others and working toward social justice."

A WORD OF CAUTION . . .

Many of the TalkSheets in this book deal with topics that may be sensitive or controversial. Discussing subjects such as sexuality or even materialism may not be appreciated by everyone in the church. Whenever you encourage discussion on such topics or encourage young people to express their opinions (on any subject), no matter how "off base" they may be, you risk the possibility of criticism from parents or other concerned adults in your church. They may believe you are teaching the youth group heresy or questionable values.

The best way to avoid problems is to use good judgment. If you have reason to believe a particular TalkSheet is going to cause problems, it would be judicious to think twice before you use it. Sometimes the damage done by going ahead outweighs the potential good.

Another way to avoid misunderstandings is to provide parents and others to whom you are accountable copies of the TalkSheet before you use it. Let them know what you hope to accomplish and the type of discussion you will be encouraging.

It would also be wise to suggest your young people take their TalkSheets home to discuss them with their parents. They might want to ask their parents how they would answer some of the questions.

CALLED TO REBEL

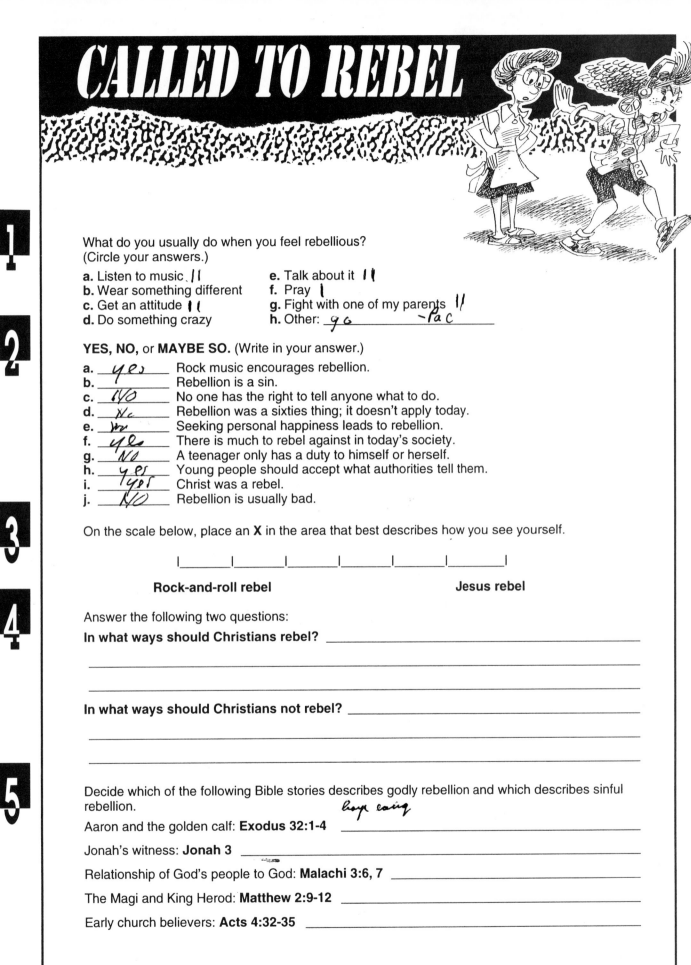

1

What do you usually do when you feel rebellious?
(Circle your answers.)

a. Listen to music ⎸⎸
b. Wear something different
c. Get an attitude ⎸⎸
d. Do something crazy

e. Talk about it ⎸⎸
f. Pray ⎸
g. Fight with one of my parents ⎸⎸
h. Other: _go ～Pac_

2

YES, NO, or **MAYBE SO.** (Write in your answer.)

a. _yes_ Rock music encourages rebellion.
b. _?_ Rebellion is a sin.
c. _No_ No one has the right to tell anyone what to do.
d. _Nc_ Rebellion was a sixties thing; it doesn't apply today.
e. _m_ Seeking personal happiness leads to rebellion.
f. _yes_ There is much to rebel against in today's society.
g. _No_ A teenager only has a duty to himself or herself.
h. _yes_ Young people should accept what authorities tell them.
i. _yes_ Christ was a rebel.
j. _No_ Rebellion is usually bad.

3

On the scale below, place an **X** in the area that best describes how you see yourself.

|_____|_____|_____|_____|_____|_____|_____|

    Rock-and-roll rebel   **Jesus rebel**

4

Answer the following two questions:

In what ways should Christians rebel? _____

_____

_____

In what ways should Christians not rebel? _____

_____

_____

5

Decide which of the following Bible stories describes godly rebellion and which describes sinful rebellion.

Aaron and the golden calf: **Exodus 32:1-4** _____

Jonah's witness: **Jonah 3** _____

Relationship of God's people to God: **Malachi 3:6, 7** _____

The Magi and King Herod: **Matthew 2:9-12** _____

Early church believers: **Acts 4:32-35** _____

Date Used: _____

Group: _____

CALLED TO REBEL
Topic: Teenage Rebellion

Purpose of this Session:

Culturally, teenagers are presented as disobedient, stubborn, uncooperative, delinquent, oppositional, and defiant—descriptive words for rebellion. A myth that persists about the adolescent years is that rebellion is normative behavior. But this is simply not true. Most teenagers do not rebel; they simply buy into the dominant cultural values that exist within their communities. Some teenagers, however, do exhibit a sort of lawless rebellion that is many a parent's nightmare. Given the state of society, it is surprising that more teenagers do not rebel against the prevailing value system. Rebellion of this sort is what Christ called his disciples to. This TalkSheet provides the opportunity to discuss both the good and the bad aspects of rebellion.

To Introduce the Topic:

Ask each group member to think of the most rebellious song with which he or she is familiar. List the various responses group members give on the chalkboard or on newsprint. When a good number of responses have been recorded, ask the group to identify the song or songs it listed that have had the most impact on young people and explain why.

Another introductory strategy would be to place between 12 to 20 pennies in a box and pass it around the group. Instruct group members to count the pennies in the box and remember how many they counted. They are not to announce how many were in the box until everyone has counted. Keep the box moving. By prior arrangement, the next to the last person secretly removes one penny from the box. In most cases the last person will conform to the group standard even though she or he totaled one less penny than the rest of the group. This provides you with a lead-in to the discussion on rebellion and conformity.

The Discussion:

Item #1: You can follow up this question by asking the group members when they usually feel the most rebellious and why.

Item #2: Ask for a Yes, No, or Maybe So vote. If everyone agrees on a particular statement, move on to the next. If there are many different opinions, ask the kids to defend their points of view. Item "a" is usually quite controversial, since most teenagers enjoy rock music. Talk about the good as well as the bad in rock music. This helps young people discern the anti-Christian from the more benign music. Item "i" offers the opportunity to talk about true discipleship. God has called Christians to a higher calling. God's kingdom turns the world's standards upside down.

Item #3: If the young people are not clear on this item, give them some examples of rebellion like dropping out of school, fighting with parents, helping the poor, doing drugs, or fighting injustice.

Item #4: Ask the students if they are rebelling in Christian ways or if they are conforming to the anti-Christian influences in society.

Item #5: Discuss how each of the stories relates to rebellion today.

To Close the Session:

Summarize the different points discussed to distinguish the two types of rebellion—Christian and sinful. Point out that all of us have rebelled against God. Fortunately God provided a way back to him through the sacrifice of his Son (Romans 5:6-8; Ephesians 2:14-18). Move on to tell the group that followers of Christ are asked to rebel against the sinful pattern of the world and conform to Christ (James 4:4).

Outside Activity:

Ask the young people to interview different church members by asking the following question: "When should Christians rebel and when should they conform?" Compare interview responses and discuss with the kids what they learned.

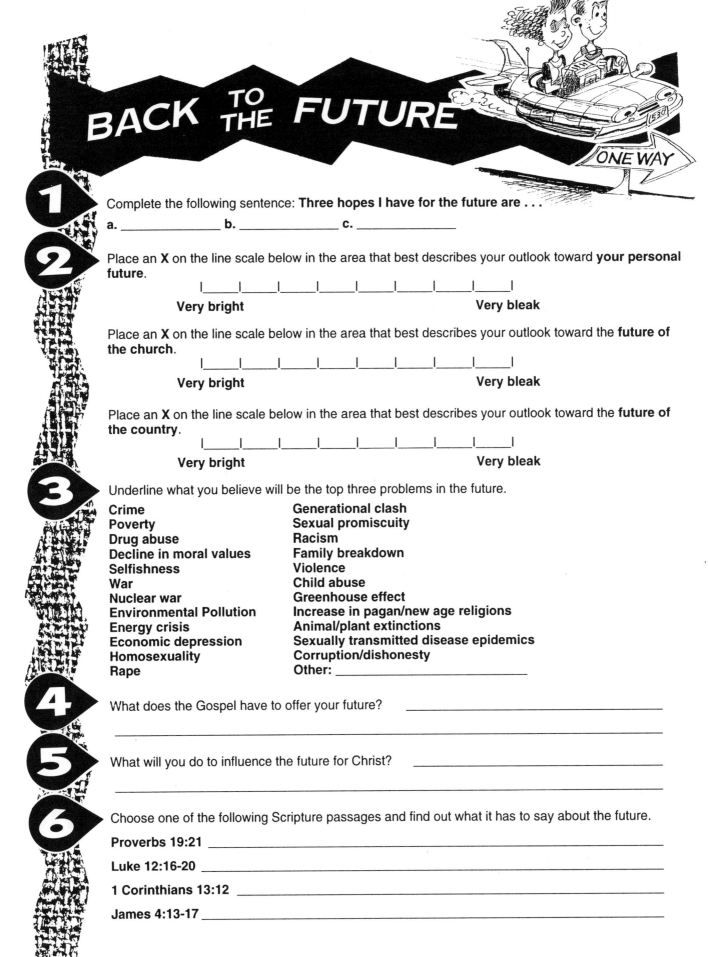

BACK TO THE FUTURE

1 Complete the following sentence: **Three hopes I have for the future are . . .**
a. _____ b. _____ c. _____

2 Place an **X** on the line scale below in the area that best describes your outlook toward **your personal future**.

|____|____|____|____|____|____|____|____|____|

Very bright   **Very bleak**

Place an **X** on the line scale below in the area that best describes your outlook toward the **future of the church**.

|____|____|____|____|____|____|____|____|____|

Very bright   **Very bleak**

Place an **X** on the line scale below in the area that best describes your outlook toward the **future of the country**.

|____|____|____|____|____|____|____|____|____|

Very bright   **Very bleak**

3 Underline what you believe will be the top three problems in the future.

Crime   **Generational clash**
Poverty   **Sexual promiscuity**
Drug abuse   **Racism**
Decline in moral values   **Family breakdown**
Selfishness   **Violence**
War   **Child abuse**
Nuclear war   **Greenhouse effect**
Environmental Pollution   **Increase in pagan/new age religions**
Energy crisis   **Animal/plant extinctions**
Economic depression   **Sexually transmitted disease epidemics**
Homosexuality   **Corruption/dishonesty**
Rape   **Other: _____**

4 What does the Gospel have to offer your future?   _____
_____

5 What will you do to influence the future for Christ?   _____
_____

6 Choose one of the following Scripture passages and find out what it has to say about the future.

Proverbs 19:21 _____

Luke 12:16-20 _____

1 Corinthians 13:12 _____

James 4:13-17 _____

Date Used: _____

Group: _____

BACK TO THE FUTURE
Topic: The Future

Purpose of this Session:

When asked by adults to describe the future, young people often mention the bright technological advances that the future will bring, but then they describe a bleak economic, moral, and environmental picture. Youths are fearful of the future in general, even if they believe that their personal futures are hopeful. This TalkSheet offers an opportunity to discuss the hope and help Christ can bring to a pessimistic generation.

To Introduce the Topic:

Pass out paper and pens to the group members. Ask them to take a couple of minutes to describe how they see themselves in ten years. Tell them to conceal their identities but to make it as true as they think it will be. Collect the descriptions and read them aloud, one at a time. After you finish reading each one, ask the group to guess the identity of each of the authors. Take a vote and let the group come to a consensus about whose future has been most accurately described. Have the author confess and briefly explain why he or she sees the future as it was described.

The Discussion:

Item #1: As a group, rank the order of everyone's hopes for the future from top to bottom. A possible ranking follows:

#1—To have a strong relationship with God.
#2—To make a good living.
#3—To get a good education.
#4—To not get a divorce.
#5—To have a great family life.

#6—To make lots of friends.
#7—To have a good time.
#8—To be of service to others.
#9—That the country will not go downhill.

You can then ask them to rank future hopes the way their non-Christian friends would rank them. Compare the two rankings and talk about the differences between Christian and non-Christian hopes for the future.

Item #2: Normally the personal futures of young people are reported as brighter than the future of the church or the country. Talk about why there is a difference. Focus on how the group feels it can impact the church positively and thus impact the country for Christ. Let the kids air their grievances about the future, but balance this with a positive perspective.

Item #3: Considerable time can be spent debating the problems foreseen in the future. Have group members describe why they chose the problems they did. See if you can reach a group consensus about the top three problems.

Item #4: Many young people believe that economic security will be their security for the future. Contrast this with the Gospel message that points to a relationship with Christ as the only hope for the future.

Item #5: This item provides an opportunity to break through the pessimism and apathy of the present generation. Unfortunately, adults have communicated to today's young people an entitlement mentality by which kids believe they have the right to a happy and economically secure future. They will do something to improve the world *if* they get paid for it.

Item #6: Let the group share its discoveries from these Scripture passages.

To Close the Session:

Explain to the group that the God we serve is the God of the past, the present, and the future. He is in control of all history, even the history of tomorrow. In serving God we may not know the future, but because we know the God of the future, we can be confident that all will work out according to God's plan (Romans 8:28).

You may want to go back to the group ranking of Item #1 and challenge the group to a serious commitment to Christ in the future. If Christ or a relationship with God is a number one hope for the future, how do they actualize this? If not, then what hope do they have without Christ?

Outside Activity:

Choose a problem from Item #3 and decide how the group can make a future difference for Christ right now.

CREATION CANCELLATION

1 Do you know someone who has had an abortion?
(Do not give any names.)

___ Yes, I know someone personally.
___ Yes, I know a friend who knows someone who had one.
___ Yes, I know it has happened with girls at my school.
___ No.

2 What do you think? (Circle one opinion for each statement.)

SA = STRONGLY AGREE   **A = AGREE**
D = DISAGREE   **SD = STRONGLY DISAGREE**

a. A woman should have a legally guaranteed right to determine what she does with her body.	SA A D SD
b. Life begins at conception.	SA A D SD
c. Abortion is murder.	SA A D SD
d. The father should have some say in the mother's decision to have an abortion.	SA A D SD
e. Safe, legal abortions are better than dangerous, illegal back-room abortions.	SA A D SD
f. Abortion is a necessary evil.	SA A D SD
g. Since there are no direct, specific guidelines in the Bible regarding abortion, Christians should not take a stand on this polarizing issue.	SA A D SD
h. The availability of the abortion pill (RU 486) should be restricted.	SA A D SD
i. Abortion is all right for others, but I don't believe in it myself.	SA A D SD

3 Place an **X** beside the statements below with which you disagree.

ABORTION SHOULD BE AVAILABLE FOR THE FOLLOWING:

A pregnant 12-year-old   **When Down's syndrome is discovered**
A drug-addicted mother   **A pregnant 26-year-old single career woman**
When the health of the mother is in danger   **A rape case**
An AIDS-infected pregnant woman   **A pregnant mother on welfare**

4 Janice is only 15 years old. She found out two weeks ago that she is pregnant. Her first thought was to terminate her pregnancy—an abortion. She is only a teenager! She definitely feels unprepared to be a mother. No way does she want to get married to the father. And adoption—how could she live with herself? It is all so confusing.

What would you want to say to Janice? _____

_____

5 Read the following Scripture verses and write out what you think each verse has to say about abortion.

Genesis 1:27 _____

Exodus 20:13 _____

Job 10:8-12 _____

Psalm 139:13-16 _____

Date Used: _____

Group: _____

CREATION CANCELLATION
Topic: Abortion

Purpose of this Session:

Abortion is a controversial and hotly debated topic. This, however, is no excuse for Christians to remove themselves from the debate. The problem of abortion will not go away. Two clearly defined camps do battle daily over this issue—the pro-choice and the pro-life movements. Most Americans fall somewhere in between the two. They have mixed feelings about abortion. They do not like it, yet they reluctantly approve of it as a necessary evil. This TalkSheet provides your group with a structured opportunity to debate the abortion issue.

To Introduce the Topic:

Place two chairs opposite each other in front of the group. Hang signs on both chairs so all the group can see them. One sign should say "Pro-life" and the other should say "Pro-choice." A single designated debater switches back and forth between the chairs. When sitting in the pro-life chair, the debater advocates that position. After 30 seconds or so, the debater switches chairs and begins advocating the pro-choice position.

The Discussion:

Item #1: Ask for a show of hands of those who answered yes. This will give you an idea of how many young people have personally encountered the issue of abortion. Be very sensitive, because some of your group members may have had abortions or had girlfriends who had one.

Item #2: No other subject creates a more heated debate than the issue of abortion. Because the abortion issue involves fundamental beliefs, it is easy to become judgmental of those with opposing opinions. Let the group members express their honest opinions. Allow for dissenting opinions. It is not necessary for you to have "the final answer" to each one. It may even be best not to share your opinions until the close of the session. Allow the young people's minds to stretch by discussing and arguing their cases with each other.

Item #3: This activity focuses upon a fundamental issue in this debate—the circumstances and the reasons behind the need for an abortion. Polls of the American public suggest that most are opposed to abortion for the purpose of birth control but support it in difficult situations. Whatever your beliefs, the circumstances and the reasons behind the need for an abortion should be addressed. The reasons can be separated into "soft" and "hard" reasons. The soft reasons include, but are not limited to, a) if a mother is using abortion as birth control, b) when a mother already has too many children, c) if a mother is unmarried, and d) when the mother cannot afford a child. The hard reasons include, but are not limited to, a) if the pregnancy resulted from incest or a rape, b) if a profound birth defect is discovered in the fetus, and c) when the health of the mother is placed in jeopardy. This activity gives you the chance to explore both the soft and the hard reasons for abortion.

Item #4: Talk with the group about the ministry opportunities that may result from crisis pregnancies. If time allows, role-play several situations.

Item #5: Ask the students to share their interpretations of these Scriptures as they relate to the issue of abortion.

To Close the Session:

At the risk of angering and alienating some readers (which I do not want to do), I will make the following observation: In general, those vehemently opposed to abortion do not compassionately concern themselves with mothers and fathers faced with a hard choice discussed in Item #3. Those advocating abortion on demand refuse to look at the fact that most abortions are for the purpose of birth control and convenience, the soft choices discussed in Item #3. Whatever your views, you need to take a biblical look at both the hard and the soft reasons for abortion, and your concluding remarks need to deal with both.

Outside Activity:

Most communities have agencies or representatives that advocate pro-life or pro-choice agendas. Assign group members the task of obtaining materials from both camps, reviewing these materials, and reporting back to the group what they learned. The group can then search the Scriptures to determine which of the positions is supported by the Bible.
Note to Leader: The abortion pill, RU 486, which causes a miscarriage, may make abortion as close as a glass of water and a little pill. The pro-life struggle could be circumvented if a black market for the pill develops or the pill is made legal in America. This will profoundly change the way the right-to-life movement advocates for the rights of the unborn.

GOING CRAZY WITH GOD

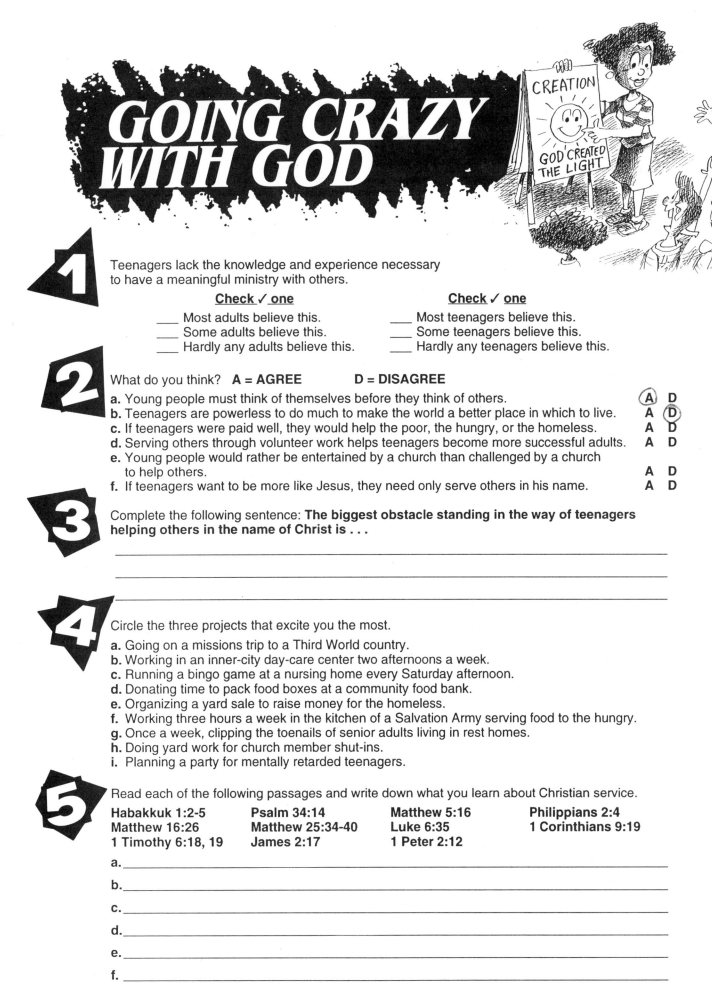

1
Teenagers lack the knowledge and experience necessary to have a meaningful ministry with others.

__Check ✓ one__	__Check ✓ one__
___ Most adults believe this.	___ Most teenagers believe this.
___ Some adults believe this.	___ Some teenagers believe this.
___ Hardly any adults believe this.	___ Hardly any teenagers believe this.

2
What do you think?   **A = AGREE**   **D = DISAGREE**

a. Young people must think of themselves before they think of others.   (A) D
b. Teenagers are powerless to do much to make the world a better place in which to live.   A (D)
c. If teenagers were paid well, they would help the poor, the hungry, or the homeless.   A D
d. Serving others through volunteer work helps teenagers become more successful adults.   A D
e. Young people would rather be entertained by a church than challenged by a church
to help others.   A D
f. If teenagers want to be more like Jesus, they need only serve others in his name.   A D

3
Complete the following sentence: **The biggest obstacle standing in the way of teenagers helping others in the name of Christ is . . .**

_____

_____

_____

4
Circle the three projects that excite you the most.

a. Going on a missions trip to a Third World country.
b. Working in an inner-city day-care center two afternoons a week.
c. Running a bingo game at a nursing home every Saturday afternoon.
d. Donating time to pack food boxes at a community food bank.
e. Organizing a yard sale to raise money for the homeless.
f. Working three hours a week in the kitchen of a Salvation Army serving food to the hungry.
g. Once a week, clipping the toenails of senior adults living in rest homes.
h. Doing yard work for church member shut-ins.
i. Planning a party for mentally retarded teenagers.

5
Read each of the following passages and write down what you learn about Christian service.

Habakkuk 1:2-5	**Psalm 34:14**	**Matthew 5:16**	**Philippians 2:4**
Matthew 16:26	**Matthew 25:34-40**	**Luke 6:35**	**1 Corinthians 9:19**
1 Timothy 6:18, 19	**James 2:17**	**1 Peter 2:12**	

a. _____

b. _____

c. _____

d. _____

e. _____

f. _____

Date Used: _____

Group: _____

GOING CRAZY WITH GOD
Topic: Christian Service

Purpose of this Session:

Christian service was an active part of church life for young people in the days of our grandparents and great-grandparents. Wayne Rice, in the preface to the book *Ideas for Social Action,* quotes Anthony Campolo: "One thing we don't need are more idea books full of games and silly social activities for youth groups! What we need is an idea book on Christian social action!" This TalkSheet helps you to focus your group's attention on the awesome opportunities that await Christians willing to serve the Lord. Use this TalkSheet time as a Christian service challenge with your group.

To Introduce the Topic:

Bring several days' worth of local newspapers to your group meeting so that the students can identify needs in your area. Break up into small groups. Give each group several newspapers. Tell the group members to look through and choose articles of local interest that identify a need in your community. Each group should then pick one article from those the kids identified. Have each group define the need presented in the article, list the possible alternative solutions and resources that would meet this need, and choose a specific way to meet the need. When all the groups are finished, have them gather together. Have a spokesperson from each group stand and present its research findings. The need as well as the group's solution and resources should be written on a chalkboard or on newsprint for the group to see. Have the large group discuss whether or not the needs of the community can be met using ideas proposed by the group.

The Discussion:

Item #1: Teenagers are often treated as objects rather than as resources who can help others. Ask the students why they believe teenagers are not consulted and utilized more in helping others.

Item #2: Poll the answers to each of the statements. If everyone agrees on a particular one, go on to the next. If there is a difference of opinion, have a pro and con discussion.

Item #3: Allow the young people to volunteer their completed sentences with the group. Ask how the identified obstacles could be removed.

Item #4: Ask the group if any of these projects should not be done by a Christian.

Item #5: Create a master list of what the group learned about Christian service. Focus on two or three of the passages for group discussion.

To Close the Session:

The Gospel is more than an individual proclaiming repentance and belief in the risen Savior who can forgive sin. The Gospel has a social dimension. The concept of the social Gospel prominent in much of mainline Protestantism in America was based on the nineteenth-century Great Awakening. Christians desired to proclaim the love of Christ through their actions. They saw how sin had manifested itself through economic injustice. They sought to stand up for Christ and say no to sin by fighting oppression. Explain to the group that the Christian life is an adventure that is more than a personal transformation. As Anthony Campolo points out, Christ is also the transformer of society. Sin affects more than just individuals—it permeates all of society. And Christians are called to work for the good of mankind (Titus 2:7; 3:8). You can close by reading Matthew 25:31-46.

Outside Activities:

1. There are many great ideas for service projects in the book *Ideas for Social Action* by Anthony Campolo (Youth Specialties/Zondervan, 1983).

2. Choose a need that was identified in the introductory activity and take this on as a group project.

PRIORITY PUZZLE

1 What is the *second* most important thing in your life?

_____

2 Here's your chance to "buy your priorities." You have 50 cents to spend. How will you spend it?

Each of these costs six cents:
○ Having a job
○ Being a radical disciple of Christ
○ Having a good time
○ Improving my looks
○ Wearing the right clothes
○ Studying hard
○ Owning a car
○ Being a leader in the church

Each of these costs five cents:
○ Attending church regularly
○ Consistently participating in youth group
○ Telling others about Christ
○ Volunteering service to help others
○ Staying active in sports
○ Regularly studying the Bible
○ Participating in extracurricular school activities

Each of these costs four cents:
○ Watching music videos
○ Turning my homework in on time
○ Helping other teenagers
○ Buying music cassettes/CDs
○ Working on my musical talent
○ Having a boyfriend/girlfriend

Each of these costs three cents:
○ Keeping a best friend
○ Going out on Saturday nights
○ Getting along with my parents
○ Spending time with my friends
○ Staying in shape

Each of these costs two cents:
○ Remaining alcohol/drug free
○ Hanging out with friends
○ Having Christian friends
○ Praying every day

Each of these costs one cent:
○ Watching TV
○ Getting to class on time
○ Going to the mall

3 Complete the following sentence: **In the next two years my priorities will change to . . .**

_____

_____

4 Which is worse—God not at all a priority in one's life or God as a low priority in one's life?
❑ **God not at all a priority**
❑ **God low on the priority list**

5 Look up the following Bible verses and complete the sentences.

2 Chronicles 1:11, 12 When you get your priorities right, then . . . _____

_____

Proverbs 3:6 When your priorities recognize God, then . . . _____

_____

Titus 1:16 Our actions demonstrate our priorities by . . . _____

_____

Revelation 3:14-18 Choose God's priorities because . . . _____

_____

Date Used: _____

Group: _____

PRIORITY PUZZLE
Topic: Priorities

Purpose of this Session:

This TalkSheet takes an honest look at young people's priorities. In a culture that pulls young people in all directions, take time to help your kids see why God needs to be in the center of their lives and priorities.

To Introduce the Topic:

Play a guessing game to prime the group to talk about priorities. On a piece of paper, have each person write his or her answers to the following questions:

In ten years . . .

1. Will you be married? Yes or No
2. What kind of career will you have pursued?
3. What kind of relationship will you have with a church?
4. What will your family-life priorities be?

Have the group sit in a circle with a volunteer who is "It" sitting in the middle. The young people in the group try to guess how the person who is "It" answered the questions.

Another way to begin the session is to ask the kids to list everything that is on and in their lockers at school. Break into groups of four, and have each group create a list of items. Then ask each group to share what it learned about what is important to its group members.

The Discussion:

Item #1: For one to identify the second most important thing in life, one must also identify number one. Ask the group members to name what is first in their lives. Then ask how the top two things in their lives affect their daily activities.

Item #2: Ask several young people to describe the priorities they "bought" for 50 cents. Concentrate the discussion on which priorities most kids bought and how they made their choices. Ask if the relative money values given to the various priorities were accurate.

Item #3: Begin the discussion of this item by first examining how the students' priorities have changed in the last two years. Include a review of where they placed God in their priorities. Then examine the upcoming two years, again including where God will fit into their future priorities. Get very specific with examples from kids' lives.

Item #4: Some young people may say that this is not a fair question, yet this is reality. Talk about how God can be moved from a low priority to a number one priority.

Item #5: This exercise contrasts the world's view of priorities with God's view. Each passage views God as the beginning and the ending points of priorities. Point out the often sharp contrast between what the Bible says and what the world says. Have the students share their completed sentences.

To Close the Session:

Point out that priorities can be easy to set but hard to live by. They need to be set in our hearts. Matthew 6:21 could be paraphrased to say, "For where your priorities are, there your heart will be also." As we daily live out our priorities, they become etched on our hearts. We should look at how we live if we want to really examine our priorities. As Christians we are new creatures called to live new lives.

Outside Activity:

Have a "New Year's in July" or whatever month it is you are using this TalkSheet. Break the young people up into groups of three or four. Ask the kids to write down New Year's resolutions in the form of priorities they would like to keep. Have them share their listed priorities.

DO CHEATERS SOMETIMES PROSPER?

1 Estimate the percentage of high school students at your school who cheat. (Circle one.)

   10%   20%   30%   40%   50%   60%   70%   80%   90%   100%

2 Rank the order of the following reasons students cheat (1 = the best; 8 = the worst).

_____ Laziness
_____ Not enough time to study
_____ Pressure to get good grades
_____ Afraid of failing
_____ Need to graduate
_____ Competition for college entrance
_____ Everybody else does it
_____ Other: _____

3 What do you think? **TRUE** or **FALSE**.

a. Boys cheat more than girls.	TRUE	FALSE
b. Adults cheat in life as much as students cheat in school.	TRUE	FALSE
c. Non-Christians cheat more than Christians.	TRUE	FALSE
d. Cheating is worth the risks.	TRUE	FALSE
e. There are times when a student has to cheat.	TRUE	FALSE

4 Is it cheating?

	SERIOUS CHEATING	BARELY CHEATING	NOT AT ALL CHEATING
a. Copying from someone's test paper.	_____	_____	_____
b. Writing answers on your arm for a test.	_____	_____	_____
c. Getting the answers for the test from someone who took it before you did.	_____	_____	_____
d. Asking someone sitting near you for the answer to a test question.	_____	_____	_____
e. Letting a friend copy answers from your test.	_____	_____	_____
f. Telling a friend an answer to a test question.	_____	_____	_____
g. Using a test from last year as a study guide.	_____	_____	_____
h. Using a test copy misplaced by the teacher as a study guide.	_____	_____	_____
i. Glancing at your class notes during a test.	_____	_____	_____
j. Letting someone copy an answer from your homework.	_____	_____	_____
k. Copying an answer from someone else's homework.	_____	_____	_____
l. Changing an answer for someone when papers are exchanged for grading purposes.	_____	_____	_____
m. Asking someone to change an answer for you when papers are exchanged for grading purposes.	_____	_____	_____

5 If cheating is okay as long as you don't get caught, why is it not okay once you get caught?

_____

_____

6 Read **Proverbs 1:10-19** and answer the following question: **How is cheating going after ill-gotten gain and what are the consequences of doing this?**

_____

_____

Date Used: _____

Group: _____

DO CHEATERS SOMETIMES PROSPER?
Topic: Cheating

Purpose of this Session:

Young people must make moral choices every day. Cheating is one of the choices that frequently confronts them. The high school experience provides many opportunities to cheat. From homework to papers to tests, students are faced with the honesty decision—and many of these decisions are not always clear-cut. Use this TalkSheet to examine the different aspects of cheating and how a Christian student can cope.

To Introduce the Topic:

Write the following options on a chalkboard or on newsprint. Tell the young people that a teacher has placed the statement "On my honor I did not cheat on this test" at the bottom of their math tests. What will they do?

1. Don't sign it.
2. Sign it before starting the test.
3. Sign it and don't cheat.
4. Sign it and cheat anyway.
5. Have someone else sign my name.

Have the young people volunteer their responses as well as their reasoning. Announce to the group you will continue your discussion on cheating using a TalkSheet.

The Discussion:

Item #1: Assess together how prevalent the practice of cheating has become. Let the group members share their gripes about cheating, such as it gives an unfair advantage to those who cheat or some teachers make it too easy to cheat.

Item #2: These are some of the common excuses students give themselves for cheating. Create a group ranking system if you can. Then take the top excuse and decide if this reason makes cheating all right.

Item #3: Let volunteers share their responses. If there appears to be disagreement, poll the group. Allow time for the group to debate when disagreement occurs. Focus on the statement "Cheating is worth the risks." Ask the students to identify the risks.

Item #4: Many students are confused over what constitutes cheating, especially in specific situations. Each of these statements is a cheating situation. Some are examples of active cheating (Items "a," "b," "c," "d," "h," "i," "k," "m") while others are passive cheating (Items "e," "f," "g," "j," "l"). Once you have debated each statement, talk about passive and active cheating and point out that both are examples of cheating.

Item #5: Not getting caught is the moral imperative that guides many students regarding cheating. Explore why some students believe that cheating is okay as long as one does not get caught.

Item #6: Ask different volunteers to answer the question. As a group, come up with a definition of cheating. Definitions can be simple, such as taking what is not yours, getting an unfair advantage, or being a fraud.

To Close the Session:

Explain that cheating is stealing. When you cheat you take something that does not belong to you. You also pretend that you are someone you are not. Cheating gives you the illusion of power. You perceive that you are controlling your life when in fact your life is moving out of control. Cheating is a form of a lie, and one lie begets another until they catch up with you. And cheating *does* catch up with you eventually.

Outside Activity:

Have the students decide whether or not they agree with the title of this TalkSheet: Do cheaters sometimes prosper? Is the saying "cheaters never prosper" valid or invalid? Ask the group to list additional examples of young people cheating—cheating on boyfriends/girlfriends, on friends, or on parents.

SATAN, INC.

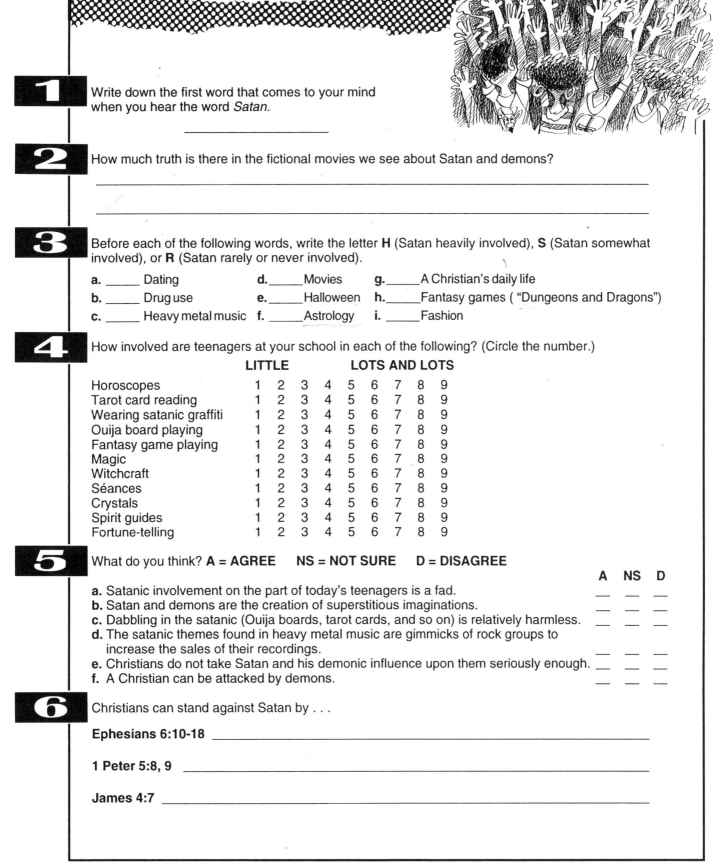

1 Write down the first word that comes to your mind when you hear the word *Satan*.

_____

2 How much truth is there in the fictional movies we see about Satan and demons?

_____

_____

3 Before each of the following words, write the letter **H** (Satan heavily involved), **S** (Satan somewhat involved), or **R** (Satan rarely or never involved).

a. _____ Dating   **d.** _____ Movies   **g.** _____ A Christian's daily life

b. _____ Drug use   **e.** _____ Halloween   **h.** _____ Fantasy games ("Dungeons and Dragons")

c. _____ Heavy metal music **f.** _____ Astrology   **i.** _____ Fashion

4 How involved are teenagers at your school in each of the following? (Circle the number.)

	LITTLE						LOTS AND LOTS	
Horoscopes	1	2	3	4	5	6	7	8	9
Tarot card reading	1	2	3	4	5	6	7	8	9
Wearing satanic graffiti	1	2	3	4	5	6	7	8	9
Ouija board playing	1	2	3	4	5	6	7	8	9
Fantasy game playing	1	2	3	4	5	6	7	8	9
Magic	1	2	3	4	5	6	7	8	9
Witchcraft	1	2	3	4	5	6	7	8	9
Séances	1	2	3	4	5	6	7	8	9
Crystals	1	2	3	4	5	6	7	8	9
Spirit guides	1	2	3	4	5	6	7	8	9
Fortune-telling	1	2	3	4	5	6	7	8	9

5 What do you think? **A = AGREE   NS = NOT SURE   D = DISAGREE**

	A	NS	D
a. Satanic involvement on the part of today's teenagers is a fad.	__	__	__
b. Satan and demons are the creation of superstitious imaginations.	__	__	__
c. Dabbling in the satanic (Ouija boards, tarot cards, and so on) is relatively harmless.	__	__	__
d. The satanic themes found in heavy metal music are gimmicks of rock groups to increase the sales of their recordings.	__	__	__
e. Christians do not take Satan and his demonic influence upon them seriously enough.	__	__	__
f. A Christian can be attacked by demons.	__	__	__

6 Christians can stand against Satan by . . .

Ephesians 6:10-18 _____

1 Peter 5:8, 9 _____

James 4:7 _____

Date Used: _____

Group: _____

SATAN, INC.
Topic: Satanism

Purpose of this Session:

C. S. Lewis wrote in *The Screwtape Letters*, "There are two equal and opposite errors into which our race can fall about the devils. One is to disbelieve in their existence. The other is to believe and to feel an excessive and unhealthy interest in them."* It is the intention of this TalkSheet to do neither, yet the tendency has been to err on either side when talking with people about satanism. The discussion that takes place should not focus upon the gory details of satanic rituals and worship but must address the realities of satanic involvement by today's high school youths. Use this TalkSheet to generate a balanced discussion on the reality of Satan in today's world.

To Introduce the Topic:

One way of quickly introducing this topic is to ask the group members to name all of the movies that contain demonic or satanic themes. You can then point out the growing trend in our culture toward the satanic.

A humorous way to begin this session is to ask two or three of the young people to create a skit. They may want to pattern the skit after the now classic "Church Lady" from *Saturday Night Live* or create their own original skit.

The Discussion:

Item #1: Write the word *Satan* on the chalkboard or on a large piece of newsprint. Ask the group members to list all of their responses. State that you would like to discuss satanism and the demonic in a mature manner without putting others down.

Item #2: On a chalkboard or on a large piece of newsprint, place two headings—"Fact" and "Fiction," with a vertical line drawn between them. Brainstorm a list of truths about Satan under the "Fact" heading and a list of falsehoods about Satan under the "Fiction" heading.

Item #3: You can expect a wide range of answers on this. Allow the group members time to debate their responses. Do not allow the debate to polarize the group, especially over the issue of heavy metal music. The point of the debate is for the group to hear different people's opinions regarding the influence Satan has in our everyday lives.

Item #4: Again you can expect a wide range of answers on this, even from those who attend the same school. This is not an attempt to discover who has the biggest problem with satanism, so do not permit names or gruesome details to be mentioned. The objective is to find out to what extent satanism is a problem. Follow up with the question, "Why do you think satanism is such a growing phenomenon?"

Item #5: These statements should generate some good, healthy debates. Have the group members share their opinions on each one and give reasons why they feel the way they do. See if the group can come to a consensus of opinion regarding Satan's influence on today's high schoolers. Focus the discussion not only on satanic activities like Ouija boards or witchcraft, but also on how Satan and evil attempt to subvert the work of Christ in today's world.

Item #6: This activity provides you with the opportunity to discuss how Christians can resist and thwart the work of the Adversary. Divide the young people into small groups and have each group take a different passage of Scripture. Allow enough time for them to reach a consensus on what they think the passage has to say about how a Christian should respond to the Devil. Each of the small groups can then report back to the group as a whole.

To Close the Session:

Explain to the group that one of Satan's strategies is to convince people he does not exist. The other strategy is to convince people he is real and that he can provide them with power. This is appealing to some young people, especially those who feel powerless. But this power is false and empty. Only the one true God has the power for living. Emphasize the reality of Satan and the evil work he and his demons are carrying out in today's world. This can be effectively and quickly done by pointing out some of the names the Bible has given Satan: accuser (Revelation 12:10), enemy (1 Peter 5:8), evil one (1 John 5:19), liar (John 8:44), and tempter (Matthew 4:3). Also emphasize that Christ came to destroy the work of the Devil (1 John 3:8), that Christ has rescued us from Satan's power (Colossians 1:18), and that the Christ who dwells in every Christian through the Holy Spirit is greater than Satan (1 John 4:4).

Outside Activity:

Have the group search the Scriptures for examples of how biblical characters dealt with Satan.

*C. S. Lewis, *The Screwtape Letters* (New York: Macmillan, 1959 and 1961), Preface.

R.O.C.K.

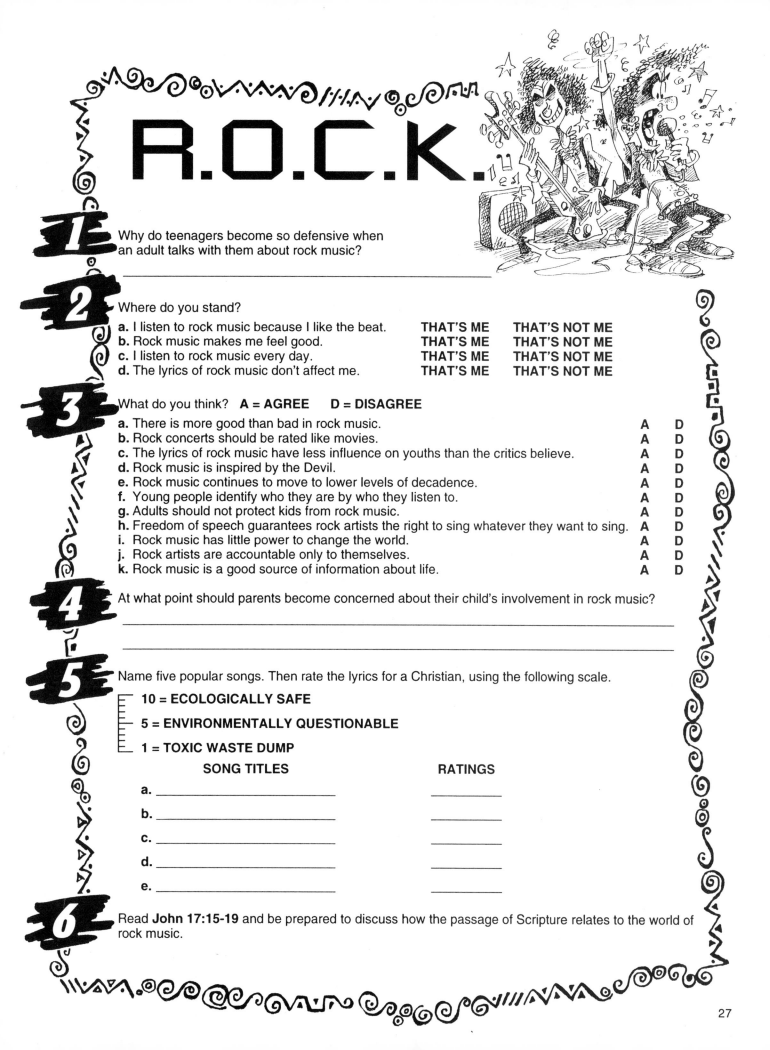

1 Why do teenagers become so defensive when an adult talks with them about rock music?

_____

2 Where do you stand?

a. I listen to rock music because I like the beat.	THAT'S ME	THAT'S NOT ME
b. Rock music makes me feel good.	THAT'S ME	THAT'S NOT ME
c. I listen to rock music every day.	THAT'S ME	THAT'S NOT ME
d. The lyrics of rock music don't affect me.	THAT'S ME	THAT'S NOT ME

3 What do you think?   **A = AGREE   D = DISAGREE**

a. There is more good than bad in rock music.	A	D
b. Rock concerts should be rated like movies.	A	D
c. The lyrics of rock music have less influence on youths than the critics believe.	A	D
d. Rock music is inspired by the Devil.	A	D
e. Rock music continues to move to lower levels of decadence.	A	D
f. Young people identify who they are by who they listen to.	A	D
g. Adults should not protect kids from rock music.	A	D
h. Freedom of speech guarantees rock artists the right to sing whatever they want to sing.	A	D
i. Rock music has little power to change the world.	A	D
j. Rock artists are accountable only to themselves.	A	D
k. Rock music is a good source of information about life.	A	D

4 At what point should parents become concerned about their child's involvement in rock music?

_____

_____

5 Name five popular songs. Then rate the lyrics for a Christian, using the following scale.

10 = ECOLOGICALLY SAFE

5 = ENVIRONMENTALLY QUESTIONABLE

1 = TOXIC WASTE DUMP

SONG TITLES	RATINGS
a. _____	_____
b. _____	_____
c. _____	_____
d. _____	_____
e. _____	_____

6 Read **John 17:15-19** and be prepared to discuss how the passage of Scripture relates to the world of rock music.

Date Used: _____

Group: _____

R.O.C.K.
Topic: Rock-and-Roll Music

Purpose of this Session:

*Rock and roll** is the one phrase that defines youth culture today. It has become an institution separated from all others, designed to impact teenagers. Rock music and the world it has created has little or nothing to do with the home, school, or church. And the home, school, and church have little to say or do with rock other than to complain about it or to condemn it. This TalkSheet has been designed to create a dialogue among youths and between youths and adult youth workers. Since there is probably no other topic that can more easily polarize a young person and an adult, the goal of this discussion should be to create a listening environment in which youths are willing to listen to the opinions of adult leaders and the adult leaders are willing to listen to the opinions of young people.

To Introduce the Topic:

Tape-record bits and pieces of some of the Top 40 hits of the month, week, or whatever. You can usually accomplish this by recording them right off the radio. Edit them so that only a second or two of each song can be heard. Then when you play the tape back for the kids, see how many of them can identify all of the songs. Usually kids are so familiar with these songs that it is nearly impossible to stump anyone, even when you only play one second of each song.

The Discussion:

Item #1: Answering this question can begin the discussion on a positive note. You can set the tone by role-modeling listening and mutual respect as you hear the responses.

Item #2: Responses to these statements will give you a basic idea of where people in your group stand. Most young people do not believe that their music affects them in negative ways, but they will point out how rock music has affected others adversely. Make a list of all of the positive things about rock music as well as all of its negative effects.

Item #3: Time usually does not permit a full discussion of each item, so ask the teens to pick five or six they wish to discuss. Item "a" is important to look at because rock concerts have degenerated to a remarkably low level. Item "k" can be examined by listing the kinds of information taught by rock music. The young people can generate a list that will help them see the deceptive values promoted by much of today's rock music.

Item #4: Encourage young people to let their parents into their rock-and-roll world. Discuss all the objections kids have about talking with their parents about rock music.

Item #5: What Christian young people need are discernment skills. This exercise can help them practice discernment. You may want to ask group members to bring specific songs to play so they can be rated by the group.

Item #6: Young people live in a rock-and-roll culture. Christ's prayer to God the Father was not that teenagers be removed from their culture but that they be protected from the Evil One. Discuss how the group can live in a rock-and-roll culture without becoming absorbed by that culture. Remind them that the Evil One is trying to have an impact upon them.

To Close the Session:

There is no quick fix solution that Christian adults can embrace to correct our young people's preoccupation with rock and roll. Slam-dunking kids with Bible verses or bashing rock personalities fails miserably. It is naive to think that rock music is innately evil. There is the good, the bad, and the ugly in rock music. Give the group your opinions about rock and roll. Challenge the teens to choose songs that can build up their faith in Jesus Christ.

Challenging questions to ask include, "What happens to you when you listen to rock?" "What Christian values does rock ridicule?" "When you listen to a rock song, are you drawn closer or further away from God?"

Here you have a wonderful opportunity to talk with your group about the variety of excellent Christian rock music available to them.

Outside Activity:

Begin a Christian rock music lending library. One or more of the young people can be in charge of setting up the library. Several kids can choose a variety of different styles of music that would appeal to your group members.

* For this TalkSheet, rock music includes rap, pop, metal, and any rock music listened to by young people today.

MOVIE MOVES

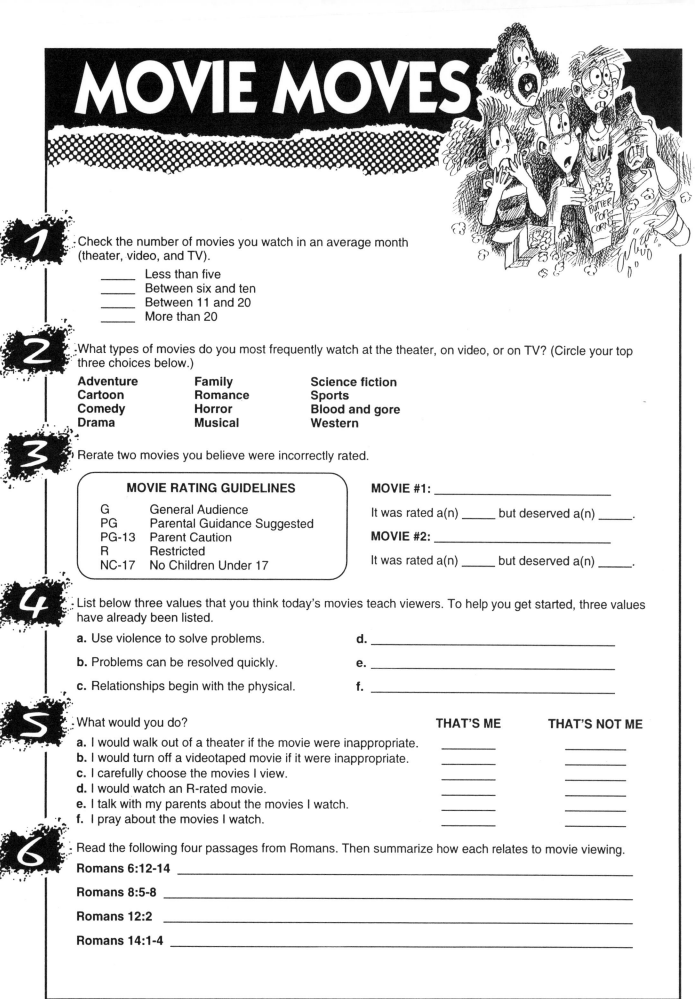

1 Check the number of movies you watch in an average month (theater, video, and TV).

_____ Less than five
_____ Between six and ten
_____ Between 11 and 20
_____ More than 20

2 What types of movies do you most frequently watch at the theater, on video, or on TV? (Circle your top three choices below.)

Adventure	**Family**	**Science fiction**
Cartoon	**Romance**	**Sports**
Comedy	**Horror**	**Blood and gore**
Drama	**Musical**	**Western**

3 Rerate two movies you believe were incorrectly rated.

MOVIE RATING GUIDELINES
G   General Audience
PG   Parental Guidance Suggested
PG-13 Parent Caution
R   Restricted
NC-17 No Children Under 17

MOVIE #1: _____

It was rated a(n) _____ but deserved a(n) _____.

MOVIE #2: _____

It was rated a(n) _____ but deserved a(n) _____.

4 List below three values that you think today's movies teach viewers. To help you get started, three values have already been listed.

a. Use violence to solve problems.

b. Problems can be resolved quickly.

c. Relationships begin with the physical.

d. _____

e. _____

f. _____

5 What would you do?

	THAT'S ME	THAT'S NOT ME
a. I would walk out of a theater if the movie were inappropriate.	_____	_____
b. I would turn off a videotaped movie if it were inappropriate.	_____	_____
c. I carefully choose the movies I view.	_____	_____
d. I would watch an R-rated movie.	_____	_____
e. I talk with my parents about the movies I watch.	_____	_____
f. I pray about the movies I watch.	_____	_____

6 Read the following four passages from Romans. Then summarize how each relates to movie viewing.

Romans 6:12-14 _____

Romans 8:5-8 _____

Romans 12:2 _____

Romans 14:1-4 _____

Date Used: _____

Group: _____

MOVIE MOVES
Topic: Movies

Purpose of this Session:

Movie viewing is now a normal part of growing up. The VCR rental movie has made unedited movie viewers of nearly all young people. This has taken place in an age where movie rating guidelines mean less and less. What was once rated an "X" now qualifies as an "R" or even a "PG." Young people today have more movie choices than ever at their rental card fingertips. And they often make their choices for all the wrong reasons. This TalkSheet provides you with the opportunity to talk about the kinds of movies your group members are viewing.

To Introduce the Topic:

Play "Charades" using recent movies. You can create a rule that the movie had to have been released within the last five to ten years. Ask every group member to write down the name of a movie on a slip of paper. Players should not see what the others have written. Collect the slips and screen for appropriateness—no X-rated stuff. Each team then draws a movie title from the pile. The teams are given three minutes to work out a scene from the movie. Reassemble the teams and let each one act out its silent scene. When the team acting is finished, the other teams guess which movie the scene was from.

The Discussion:

Item #1: Obtain a group average for a month. Then let the students estimate how many movies they will have watched by the time they graduate from high school. Make the observation that the group puts a lot of time into movie viewing.

Item #2: Ask several group members to share their top three movie choices. This will give you an idea of the kinds of movies your group is viewing. In order to get a parental perspective, ask the kids how many of the movies they have watched would win their parents' seals of approval.

Item #3: You may have to explain this activity to some of your group members. The easiest way to do so is through an example from your own movie viewing experience. The point of this activity is threefold. 1) It will help kids become more aware of the reason for a rating system. Ask the group to share some of its ratings. Point out that movies receive different ratings because their moral content differs. 2) It will help kids discern good from bad moral content. Ask the group to share the reasons for its ratings. You will get a variety of responses depending upon the types of movies the kids chose to rate. 3) It will help kids create their own Christian rating system. Ask the group to create a list of all the reasons for rating a movie NC-17, R, PG-13, PG, and G. You will get answers like violence, foul language, sex, nudity, and so on. Now challenge the kids to create their own rating system that God would approve of. Apply this new rating system to several of the movies that the kids listed in Item #2.

Item #4: Create a group list of all the young people's responses. Compare the list to see how many good values are taught versus how many bad values are taught. Ask the students to explain how they can watch movies without being affected by the bad values.

Item #5: Here is an opportunity for kids to personally commit or not commit to critically watching movies. After getting the students to share their answers, ask them to go back and look at the list and decide what changes they would like to make in their movie viewing.

Item #6: Ask them to read their summaries and describe one thing they learned from the book of Romans about movie viewing.

To Close the Session:

Let the kids know that they do have decisions to make when it comes to going to the theater or renting a videotaped movie. Challenge your students to talk with their parents and church leaders about movies before they decide whether or not to watch them and to apply the Christian rating system created in Item #3. If a movie is bad, they can leave the theater or turn off the VCR, something that many young people forget is an option.

Outside Activity:

Photocopy and pass out a critical movie review of a popular movie from your local newspaper or a national magazine. Ask the group to read it and decide if the movie is one that is appropriate for a Christian to view.

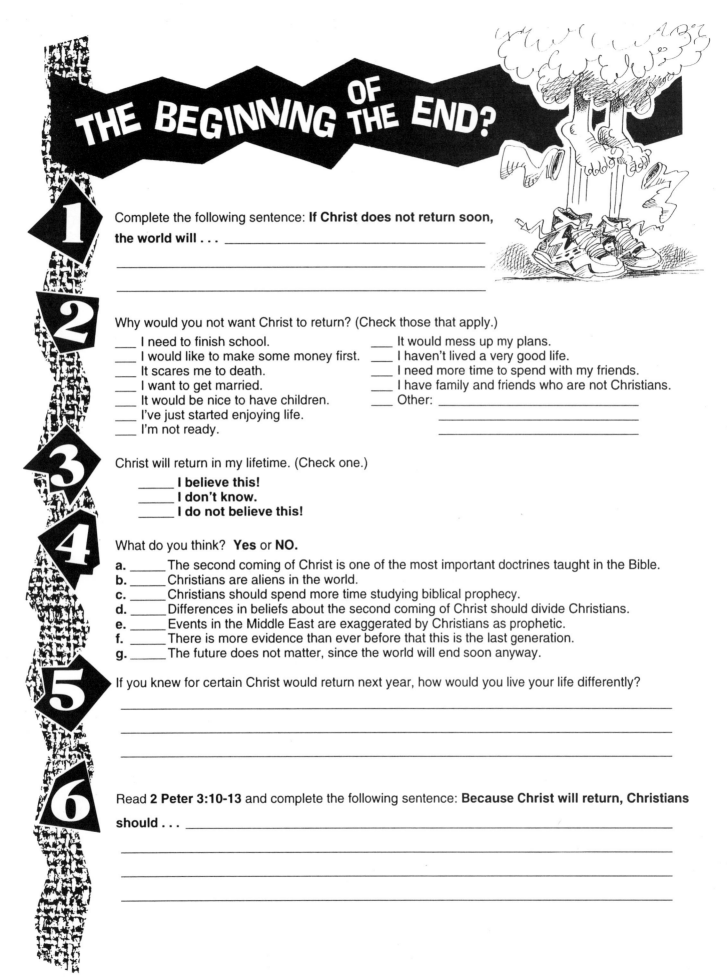

THE BEGINNING OF THE END?

1 Complete the following sentence: **If Christ does not return soon, the world will . . .** _____

_____

_____

2 Why would you not want Christ to return? (Check those that apply.)

___ I need to finish school.
___ I would like to make some money first.
___ It scares me to death.
___ I want to get married.
___ It would be nice to have children.
___ I've just started enjoying life.
___ I'm not ready.

___ It would mess up my plans.
___ I haven't lived a very good life.
___ I need more time to spend with my friends.
___ I have family and friends who are not Christians.
___ Other: _____
_____
_____

3 Christ will return in my lifetime. (Check one.)

_____ **I believe this!**
_____ **I don't know.**
_____ **I do not believe this!**

4 What do you think? **Yes** or **NO.**

a. _____ The second coming of Christ is one of the most important doctrines taught in the Bible.
b. _____ Christians are aliens in the world.
c. _____ Christians should spend more time studying biblical prophecy.
d. _____ Differences in beliefs about the second coming of Christ should divide Christians.
e. _____ Events in the Middle East are exaggerated by Christians as prophetic.
f. _____ There is more evidence than ever before that this is the last generation.
g. _____ The future does not matter, since the world will end soon anyway.

5 If you knew for certain Christ would return next year, how would you live your life differently?

_____

_____

_____

6 Read **2 Peter 3:10-13** and complete the following sentence: **Because Christ will return, Christians should . . .** _____

_____

_____

_____

_____

THE BEGINNING OF THE END?
Topic: The Second Coming of Christ

Purpose of this Session:

As we approach and enter the new century, interest in the second coming of Christ will intensify. A similar phenomenon occurred in history with the approach of the first millennium after Christ's birth. This TalkSheet provides your group with a format in which to discuss the return of Christ.

To Introduce the Topic:

The following is a spoof on the emergency broadcasting network test that is run on television and radio. Read the following to the students as they are about to be seated. Overdramatize the reading and make it fun.

"This is a test of the End Times Network. Christ has returned. This is only a test. (Blow a whistle or sound a trumpet if you have access to one.) Since this is not an actual Second Coming, you are instructed to turn to your Bible for more information."

Now ask the group the following question: "What is the first thing you thought of when you heard that Christ had returned?"

The Discussion:

Item #1: You may receive a mixed bag of predictions. Young people who are techno-friendly see advances on the technological front but will report the future decline of morality, the environment, and other social problems.

Item #2: Examine the various responses of your kids, asking why they feel the way they do.

Item #3: Ponder with the group if this generation is the culmination of history. Explain that Christ's return is not a rescue mission but the completion of history and the fulfillment of prophecy.

Item #4: Each of these statements has the potential for further discussion. If there are questions or disagreements on any of these, take the time to probe the issues. Remember that even theologians and Bible teachers cannot agree on the specifics of the Second Coming. So do not make a federal case out of any one statement.

Item #5: Postulate what it might be like if Christ returned today. What regrets might we have?

Item #6: Have the students share their views. Ask if Christ's return really matters to them in terms of the way they plan to live their lives.

To Close the Session:

Christ's first and second comings are inextricable. His coming again presupposes his death and resurrection, while the first coming would be meaningless were it not for Christ's return for those he died for. Young people need to understand that the two advents are closely linked. Immediately upon Christ's departure into heaven, his return was affirmed (Acts 1:22). Since we can be assured of Christ's return as part of our Christian hope, we can go about his business. The Bible can often appear distorted and out of touch with current reality. But an understanding of Jesus' return puts the Bible's upside down view of daily living into proper perspective. When one views life not from the beginning but from the end of history, what happens in between changes in significance.

Christ told us in his own words that no one will know when he will return (Matthew 24:36). In fact, if Christ waited another 1,000 years before coming back, not a single prophecy would go unfulfilled. What is happening today is not necessarily fulfillment of prophecy, but it could be.

Close the discussion by examining the way we are to live our lives while awaiting the "blessed hope" of his return (Titus 2:11-14).

Outside Activity:

Invite the pastor of your church to attend the group and explain the various theological views that exist regarding the Second Coming. The teens can also ask the pastor questions they have about Christ's return. Some potential questions to get the discussion going are as follows:

1. Are we living in the last days?
2. Why are there so many views of Christ's return?
3. Should we worry about our educations?
4. Why didn't Jesus tell us when he was coming back?
5. How has the doctrine of the second coming of Christ affected your life?

AIDS ALERT

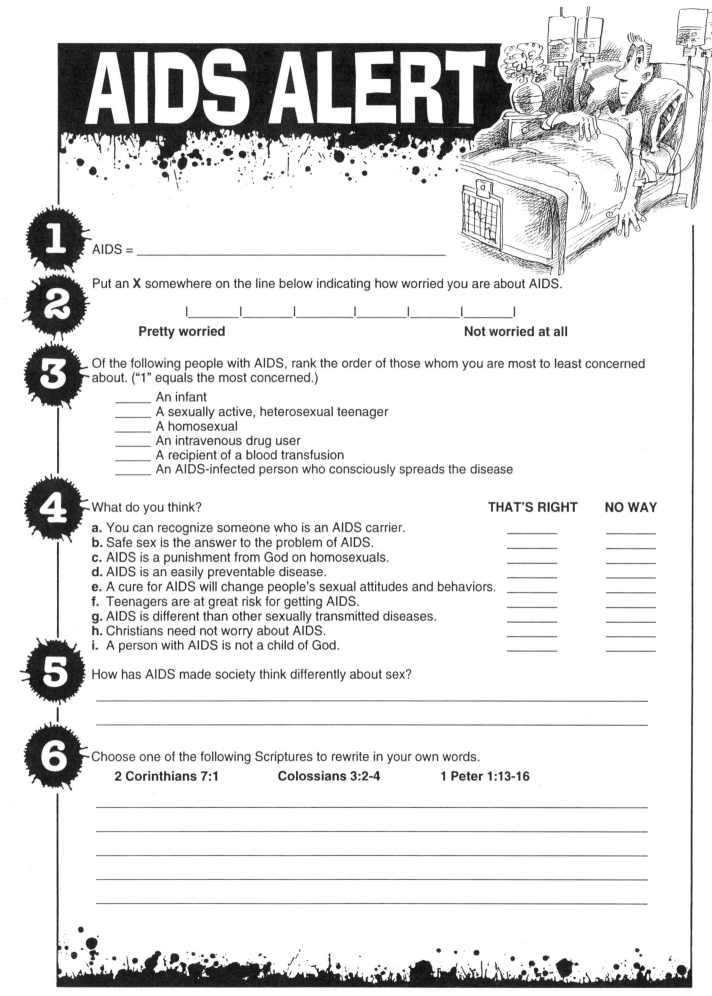

1 AIDS = _____

2 Put an **X** somewhere on the line below indicating how worried you are about AIDS.

|_____|_____|_____|_____|_____|_____|_____|

Pretty worried   **Not worried at all**

3 Of the following people with AIDS, rank the order of those whom you are most to least concerned about. ("1" equals the most concerned.)

_____ An infant
_____ A sexually active, heterosexual teenager
_____ A homosexual
_____ An intravenous drug user
_____ A recipient of a blood transfusion
_____ An AIDS-infected person who consciously spreads the disease

4 What do you think?   **THAT'S RIGHT**   **NO WAY**

a. You can recognize someone who is an AIDS carrier.   _____   _____
b. Safe sex is the answer to the problem of AIDS.   _____   _____
c. AIDS is a punishment from God on homosexuals.   _____   _____
d. AIDS is an easily preventable disease.   _____   _____
e. A cure for AIDS will change people's sexual attitudes and behaviors.   _____   _____
f. Teenagers are at great risk for getting AIDS.   _____   _____
g. AIDS is different than other sexually transmitted diseases.   _____   _____
h. Christians need not worry about AIDS.   _____   _____
i. A person with AIDS is not a child of God.   _____   _____

5 How has AIDS made society think differently about sex?

_____
_____

6 Choose one of the following Scriptures to rewrite in your own words.

2 Corinthians 7:1   **Colossians 3:2-4**   **1 Peter 1:13-16**

_____
_____
_____
_____
_____
_____

Date Used: _____

Group: _____

AIDS ALERT
Topic: AIDS

Purpose of this Session:

Young people need to know about AIDS, and they need to hear what other Christians have to say. Society has portrayed the church as homophobic and afraid of talking about AIDS. Use this TalkSheet to talk about this important issue.

To Introduce the Topic:

Take a sealed envelope and hold it up before the group. Ask the group to respond to the following question: "If this envelope contained the names of people in the group who have tested positive for the AIDS virus, would you want to know who they are?" Then explore why they would or would not want to know.

The Discussion:

Item #1: AIDS, or Acquired Immunodeficiency Syndrome, is a disease that attacks the immune system of the body. Allow the students the opportunity to share their opinions about this deadly disease.

Item #2: Focus some attention on the "not me" attitude of many people regarding AIDS.

Item #3: Talk about the compassion Christ had for those who had leprosy.

Item #4: Some comments are necessary about the statements. a.) You cannot recognize someone who has AIDS simply by looking at them. b.) Safe sex is not the answer. Abstinence for those who are single and a faithful monogamous relationship with an uninfected partner for those who are married is the best answer to stopping the sexual spread of the disease. c.) AIDS is not a punishment from God. If God wanted to immediately punish sin, we would all have been given AIDS. d.) For the most part, AIDS is a preventable disease. e.) Spend some time talking about the emphasis placed upon finding a cure rather than upon changing a lifestyle. This does not mean that a cure should not be sought. However, this is the first disease given civil rights and political clout because it interferes with a moral issue—that of permissive sexual conduct. AIDS has interfered with the sexual revolution and alternative lifestyles. The focus has been on how to continue immoral lifestyles (safe sex) rather than on abstinence. f.) Teenagers must worry about AIDS if they unwisely choose involvement in premarital sex or intravenous drug use. g.) AIDS is different because it can kill you. h.) Christians should be concerned because people with the disease, as well as their friends and loved ones, need our compassion. i.) All people are created in God's image, but not all are believers. All people need the Gospel.

Item #5: Explore the changes you and the group have noticed as a result of the AIDS epidemic. Talk about the sexual revolution of the 1960s versus how people are acting today. Has it made a difference in the way teenagers act or in the way adults act sexually?

Item #6: Ask for volunteers to read what they have written. Explore how these passages relate to AIDS.

To Close the Session:

Review the points made during the discussion. Point out that AIDS cannot be contracted from casual contact. Focus on God's love for all people, including those with AIDS. Everyone needs the Gospel, and God wants everyone to accept his free gift of salvation (2 Peter 3:9). As Christians we need to take God's love to people who have the AIDS disease or any other disease. The prejudice shown by many toward those with AIDS is homophobic and sinful. If God were punishing those with AIDS, then he has made a grave mistake, since some babies are born with the disease. All of us deserve death because of our sins, not just homosexuals (Romans 6:23).

Reemphasize that the best protection against the AIDS virus is not safe sex but abstinence from premarital sex.

Outside Activity:

You may obtain helpful information from your local Red Cross or public health department that can be used to help answer your kids' questions regarding AIDS.

TALK ISN'T THAT CHEAP

1 How often do you and one or both of your parents talk about each of the following?

	OFTEN	SOMETIMES	RARELY	NEVER
___ a. Family rules	___	___	___	___
___ b. Your future plans	___	___	___	___
___ c. Chores	___	___	___	___
___ d. Schoolwork	___	___	___	___
___ e. Family relationships or problems	___	___	___	___
___ f. Sex	___	___	___	___
___ g. Alcohol/drugs	___	___	___	___
___ h. Christianity/church	___	___	___	___
___ i. Politics	___	___	___	___
___ j. Friendships	___	___	___	___
___ k. Daily activities	___	___	___	___
___ l. Fears	___	___	___	___
___ m. Feelings	___	___	___	___
___ n. Disobedience	___	___	___	___
___ o. Your interests	___	___	___	___
___ p. Sibling problems	___	___	___	___
___ q. Your social activities	___	___	___	___
___ r. Social problems (crime, homelessness)	___	___	___	___
___ s. Your problems	___	___	___	___
___ t. Rock music	___	___	___	___

2 When you do have a talk with one or both of your parents, who usually starts the talk?

WITH MY MOTHER
_____ I usually do.
_____ My mother usually does.
_____ It is about equal between us.

WITH MY FATHER
_____ I usually do.
_____ My father usually does.
_____ It is about equal between us.

3 Go back to the first question. On the lines before each item, place an **S** if you are usually satisfied with the talk or an **A** if the talk often turns into an argument.

4 Place an **X** before each of the following issues for which you have shared your personal views with at least one of your parents.

___ a. Family rules
___ b. Your future plans
___ c. Chores
___ d. Schoolwork
___ e. Family relationships or problems
___ f. Sex
___ g. Alcohol/drugs

___ h. Christianity/church
___ i. Politics
___ j. Friendships
___ k. Fears
___ l. Feelings
___ m. Disobedience

___ n. Your interests
___ o. Sibling problems
___ p. Your social activities
___ q. Social problems (crime, homelessness)
___ r. Your problems
___ s. Rock music

5 If you could change one thing about the way you and your mom or your dad talk with each other, what would it be?

_____

_____

6 Each of the following passages relates in some way to communicating. Choose one to discuss with the group.

Job 2:13	Proverbs 2:3-6	Proverbs 15:1
2 Timothy 2:7	James 1:19	James 3:9-12

Date Used: _____/_____

Group: _____

TALK ISN'T THAT CHEAP
Topic: Parent/Teen Communication

Purpose of this Session:

This TalkSheet is about a special kind of talk—one that needs to be encouraged and nurtured. A talk you can rarely have enough of. The lack of this kind of communication between parents and their teenage children has been labeled the culprit for many family problems, not to mention societal ills. Use this TalkSheet discussion time to examine and encourage communication between your teenagers and their parents.

To Introduce the Topic:

For this introduction your group will need acting ability and a sense of humor. Tell the group it will be doing "Parent Impressions." Some of the students will get the opportunity to "act" like parents and some will "act" like average teens. Divide your kids into groups of three. Tell them to decide who will play each role in their group. The group could consist of two parents and one child, a single mom and two kids, or a dad and a stepmom with a teenager. You get the picture. Write some "Parent Impressions" titles on slips of paper and place them in a sack or a box. Have each "family" draw a title and work to develop the skit based upon the title it chose. When rehearsal time is up, have your groups focus their attention on those acting out their skits. Sit back and enjoy the creativity. The following are some sample titles:

"The Problem Phone Line"   "Dating Do's and Don'ts"   "I Don't Like Your Friends"
"Drugs Can Kill"   "Where Is Your Report Card?"   "Where Were You Tonight?"

The Discussion:

The term *parent* in the following items refers to all kinds of parents—birth, step, foster, or guardian.

Item #1: Take a poll to see which issues your teens talk most often about with their parents. Write these down for all to see. Do the same for those issues that are rarely or never discussed. Ask the students to summarize what this says about their overall communication with their parents.

Item #2: Talk about who has the responsibility for communication. Do young people have to wait for their parents? What if their parents do not want to talk or are not very good at communicating?

Item #3: Some talks begin as arguments and end satisfactorily. Others start as pleasant discussions and end in arguments. Brainstorm with the teens about how their patterns of communicating with their parents can become more satisfactory.

Item #4: Ask the group members if there are any issues they should be talking over with their parents but aren't. Summarize the group's sharing of personal views into a statement or two. For example, the students may find that the more important the issue, the less likely they are to share their personal views with their parents. Ask the group if this summary statement represents the way things should be.

Item #5: Let volunteers share their changes. See if there is a common theme among your group's responses. Ask the group members how they can bring about these changes by changing their own behaviors.

Item #6: Discuss the verses and write down on a chalkboard or on newsprint the point learned by the group.

To Close the Session:

Close by asking the group members to commit to talking to their parents about one issue found on the TalkSheet. You can have the teens sit in a circle and share their commitments before closing in prayer, or this commitment to communicate can be said in the form of a prayer.

Outside Activity:

Talk shows are a popular form of communication today. This outside activity will bring together kids and parents in a fun yet meaningful way, allowing the young people a chance to see a parental perspective. You will need four to eight parents as talk show guests, and your group members will be the audience. Allow the audience to write down questions in advance to ask the "guests"; members can also ask questions during the program. Allow your group to come up with a creative name for your show like "Fam Talk" or "The Oprah Donahue Show." Choose a talk show host from your group. A catchy theme song can be played as the guests enter; the host introduces the guests and the topic of the show. Provide the host with two or three sample questions to start off the show, like the following:

1. "Why do parents demand that there be open communication?"
2. "Why don't parents trust their teenagers?"
3. "Do you think teenagers communicate enough with their parents?"
4. "If you could tell young people only one thing about parents, what would you say?"

HARD ROCK CAFETERIA

1 If you were to interview a hard rock music group, what would be the most important question you would ask?

_____

_____

_____

2 What do you think?   **A = AGREE**   **NS = NOT SURE**   **D = DISAGREE**

	A	NS	D
a. Hard rock is a religion to its dedicated fans.	A	NS	D
b. Young people don't just listen to hard rock, they live hard rock.	A	NS	D
c. Hard rock music is merely entertainment.	A	NS	D
d. Hard rock provides positive solutions to societal problems.	A	NS	D
e. Hard rock desensitizes the listener to moral purity.	A	NS	D
f. Hard rock concerts should be more closely regulated by authorities.	A	NS	D
g. Hard rock exploits teenagers.	A	NS	D
h. There is a difference between young people who listen to rock and young people who listen to hard rock.	A	NS	D
i. Hard rock is the gospel music of the world.	A	NS	D
j. Christian hard rock influences people to listen to secular hard rock.	A	NS	D

3 Hard rock is a contributing factor to which of the following problems? (Check your answers.)

____ Rebellion	____ Suicide	____ Family conflict
____ Alcohol/drug use	____ Satanism	____ Vandalism
____ Pornography	____ Permissive sexual attitudes	____ Alienation
____ Destructive behavior	____ Exploitive sex	____ Profanity
____ Agnosticism	____ Psychological problems	____ Racism
____ Apathy	____ Violence	____ Sex-role stereotyping
____ Aggression	____ Hatred/anger	____ School difficulties
____ Spiritual decline	____ Depression	____ Risky behavior

4 Circle where you stand on the following statements:

a. I agree with the ideas stated in hard rock song lyrics. **ALWAYS OFTEN SOMETIMES NEVER**

b. I agree with the lifestyle choices of hard rock band members. **ALWAYS OFTEN SOMETIMES NEVER**

c. I agree with the way hard rock band members dress. **ALWAYS OFTEN SOMETIMES NEVER**

d. I agree with what occurs at hard rock concerts. **ALWAYS OFTEN SOMETIMES NEVER**

e. I agree with the visual images portrayed in hard rock music videos, posters, and T-shirts. **ALWAYS OFTEN SOMETIMES NEVER**

5 Read **Colossians 2:8**, then identify three deceptive philosophies or teachings promoted by hard rock music that could lead a Christian away from Christ.

Deceptive Philosophy #1 _____

Deceptive Philosophy #2 _____

Deceptive Philosophy #3 _____

Date Used: _____

Group: _____

HARD ROCK CAFETERIA
Topic: Hard Rock Music

Purpose of this Session:

Rock music has turned the corner on decency. It has been at the forefront in promoting an "anything goes" culture. The explicitness of rock and roll, much of it pushed by harder styles of rock, can be openly and honestly debated by using this TalkSheet.

To Introduce the Topic:

Rock music has always been controversial. Its primary function of offending parental sensibilities has grown increasingly more difficult as yesterday's rockers have become parents. A new genre of harder rock has shown little self-restraint as it has departed from more traditional forms of rock music. To introduce a discussion about this harder form of rock, ask the kids to define hard rock. The lyrics, band names, concert antics, dress, and stage props are generally clear giveaways as to what hard-core rock groups are really like. Create a list of rock groups that your group members consider hard rock. You can be as liberal or as conservative as your group wishes in defining hard rock.

The Discussion:

Item #1: Ask for volunteers to share their responses. This is a positive and nonthreatening way to begin your controversial discussion. You do not need to discuss the answers in depth.

Item #2: Take time to explore each of these statements. Item "a" is true in that hard rock can become a religion for some kids with the lyrics becoming a theology of hate, violence, and exploitive sex. Kids like to focus on Item "b" because so many young people either do live rock or wish they could. Talk about the consequences of living out hard rock as a philosophy of life. Item "e" is important because the explicitness of lyrics in hard rock desensitizes listeners: they can become violent and adopt permissive, defiant sexual attitudes and practices.

Item #3: In addition to these problems, young people will bring up good things. They should also be discussed. Let kids add anything they wish, both positive and negative.

Item #4: The more group members circle "ALWAYS" and "OFTEN" responses, the more likely they are to be involved in hard rock, and the more likely they are being adversely affected by it. If they circled "SOMETIMES" and "NEVER," ask them why they listen to it if it is so disagreeable.

Item #5: Create a large list of all of the deceptive philosophies being promoted by hard rock that the group identified.

To Close the Session:

Simply because the hard rock genre of music is not appreciated by adults does not mean it is innately evil. All hard rock is not satanic. At the same time, there are some very real dangers with this type of music. Frame your concluding remarks in such a manner that you give your young people something to think about, but don't alienate them. Create a list of characteristics of hard rock music as a whole (pornographic, negativistic, destructive, alienating, godless), and ask the kids if this is something that furthers the kingdom of God. Avoid rock bashing in terms of knocking specific groups. This only tends to alienate young people.

One of the strongest impacts you can have on your group is to simply summarize the points made during the discussion. Hard rock may have had its defenders during the discussion, but if you listened and respected the opinions of all participants, you most likely found most group members openly talking about the negative aspects of hard rock. Reflecting on what has been said by the kids about hard rock music will be much more powerful than anything you could say.

Outside Activity:

Rate a number of hard rock CDs/cassettes the same way movies are rated (G, PG, PG-13, R, and NC-17). Then discuss the reasons why each was given the rating it received.

HAPPILY EVER AFTER

1 How happy are you today? (Check the appropriate box.)

- ☐ 😄 **Very happy**
- ☐ 🙂 **Pretty happy**
- ☐ 🙂 **Slightly happy**
- ☐ 😐 **Neutral**
- ☐ 🙁 **Slightly unhappy**
- ☐ ☹️ **Pretty unhappy**
- ☐ 😞 **Very unhappy**

2 Happiness is . . .   (Circle your top three choices.)

A purpose in life	Salvation	Good looks
Service to others	A good job	New clothes
Material things	Good grades	Health
A positive family life	Sex	Being loved
A boyfriend/girlfriend	Popularity	Recovery
Great friends	Being young	Spending private time with God

3 What do you think? **YES, NO,** or **MAYBE SO.**

a. Happiness is an important goal in life.	YES	MAYBE	NO
b. Happiness is a mood.	YES	MAYBE	NO
c. The more money one has, the happier one is.	YES	MAYBE	NO
d. Seeking happiness leads to selfishness.	YES	MAYBE	NO
e. Not everyone can be happy.	YES	MAYBE	NO
f. Parents are responsible for their kids' happiness and unhappiness.	YES	MAYBE	NO

4 Answer each of the following questions by circling the number on the scale that matches how you feel.

	NONE OF THE TIME			HALF OF THE TIME			ALL OF THE TIME
a. How often do you feel sad?	1	2	3	4	5	6	7
b. How often do you feel lonely?	1	2	3	4	5	6	7
c. How often do you feel afraid?	1	2	3	4	5	6	7
d. How often do you feel stressed?	1	2	3	4	5	6	7
e. How often do you feel far away from God?	1	2	3	4	5	6	7
f. How often do you feel down?	1	2	3	4	5	6	7

5 I feel satisfied with the direction my life is going.

_____ **I agree**   _____ **I disagree**

6 Read the Beatitudes in **Matthew 5:1-12** and write out why you believe the people Christ described are happy (blessed). _____

_____

Date Used: _____

Group: _____

HAPPILY EVER AFTER
Topic: Happiness

Purpose of this Session:

For many who pursue it, happiness is elusive. Interestingly, the Bible has very little to say directly about happiness. Most Americans spend their lives chasing it—"life, liberty, and the pursuit of happiness." When we try to define happiness, we usually do so by describing things that do not make us happy— money, sex, work, friends, and youth. This TalkSheet can help your teens examine what their culture says about it and how God sees it.

To Introduce the Topic:

Introduce this joyous topic by holding a Cracker Jack box up before your group. Have them think back to when they were little kids and found prizes in their Cracker Jack boxes. How did this make them feel? Why did it make them happy to find a prize in the box? Ask the young people how they feel now when they see a Cracker Jack box. Does finding the prize give them the same happiness as it did when they were children? Why or why not? Discuss why their perceptions of happiness have changed as they have grown older.

An alternative introduction would be to pass out newspapers or magazines and have the students find as many examples of happiness as they can in three minutes. Ask them to share their findings.

The Discussion:

Item #1: Give the young people the chance to share their feelings and give an explanation why. Ask them how often they fake happiness.

Item #2: Ask the kids which of these things are worth living their lives around. Is the list the same as what equals happiness? Point out that the things that make life worth living are those things that bring happiness. There is, however, a paradox here. If one spends his or her life pursuing happiness (which can equal hedonism or pleasure), one will not find it. But if one spends her or his life in service to God and others, happiness will be a by-product. Happiness can never be a goal, only a by-product. Happiness is an interesting concept. People have difficulty defining it, but they can tell you when they have experienced it.

Item #3: The young people will think of additional things, so create a master list on a chalkboard or on newsprint.

Item #4: Get an overall picture by asking the kids if they see a correlation or relationship among each of the questions. For example, did the people who felt sad also report feeling far away from God?

Item #5: Ask the young people to explain their answers. Should the direction they are going stay the same or should it change? If it needs to change, are they willing to make the necessary changes?

Item #6: Carefully study the list of happy people Christ described. Does the list have much in common with what we normally consider happiness to be? It seems Jesus described happiness as something totally foreign to most. Why is God's kingdom different than the world?

To Close the Session:

Point out that people commonly describe happiness by looking outwardly at things or circumstances. But the Bible says happiness is an attitude. When Paul wrote to the Philippians, he said he had learned to be content with plenty or with little. He could do both through the strength given by Christ (Philippians 4:13). Paul had learned to rise above his circumstances because he knew that they could not provide happiness. Research demonstrates that the rich report no more happiness than the common folk. Things and circumstances cannot bring happiness. Yet we continue to play the "if only" game, believing falsely that a change in our situation will bring the happiness we desire. What Paul had come to realize is something we can learn as well. Happiness is how you view your circumstances, not your circumstances themselves. Paul learned that living under the power of Christ provided him with all he needed to be happy. He quit searching outside himself and turned upward toward God. The Bible calls this joy.

Outside Activities:

1. Have your group conduct a "Happiness Survey." Pass out five 3 x 5 cards to each young person. Ask the teens to write the following incomplete sentence on each card: **Happiness for me is . . .** During the next week, have the students get five people of different ages to complete the sentences. Each person should put his or her age, sex, and religion on the card. Have them bring the cards back to the next meeting. After all the cards are read to the group, discuss the various ways people view happiness.

2. Have the group use a concordance to search the biblical references for the word *joy*. Make a list of what they learned.

THE LEAST OF THESE

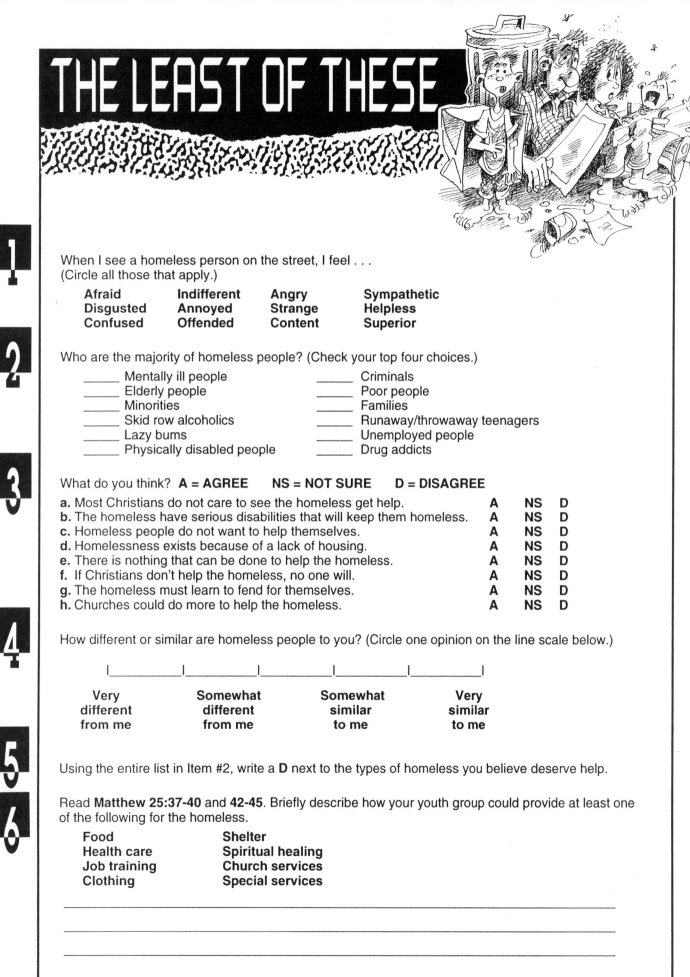

1 When I see a homeless person on the street, I feel . . .
(Circle all those that apply.)

Afraid	**Indifferent**	**Angry**	**Sympathetic**
Disgusted	**Annoyed**	**Strange**	**Helpless**
Confused	**Offended**	**Content**	**Superior**

2 Who are the majority of homeless people? (Check your top four choices.)

_____ Mentally ill people   _____ Criminals
_____ Elderly people   _____ Poor people
_____ Minorities   _____ Families
_____ Skid row alcoholics   _____ Runaway/throwaway teenagers
_____ Lazy bums   _____ Unemployed people
_____ Physically disabled people   _____ Drug addicts

3 What do you think? **A = AGREE   NS = NOT SURE   D = DISAGREE**

a. Most Christians do not care to see the homeless get help.   **A   NS   D**
b. The homeless have serious disabilities that will keep them homeless.   **A   NS   D**
c. Homeless people do not want to help themselves.   **A   NS   D**
d. Homelessness exists because of a lack of housing.   **A   NS   D**
e. There is nothing that can be done to help the homeless.   **A   NS   D**
f. If Christians don't help the homeless, no one will.   **A   NS   D**
g. The homeless must learn to fend for themselves.   **A   NS   D**
h. Churches could do more to help the homeless.   **A   NS   D**

4 How different or similar are homeless people to you? (Circle one opinion on the line scale below.)

|_____|_____|_____|_____|_____|_____|

Very	**Somewhat**	**Somewhat**	**Very**
different	**different**	**similar**	**similar**
from me	**from me**	**to me**	**to me**

5 Using the entire list in Item #2, write a **D** next to the types of homeless you believe deserve help.

6 Read **Matthew 25:37-40** and **42-45**. Briefly describe how your youth group could provide at least one of the following for the homeless.

Food	**Shelter**
Health care	**Spiritual healing**
Job training	**Church services**
Clothing	**Special services**

_____

_____

_____

Date Used:_____

Group:_____

THE LEAST OF THESE
Topic: The Homeless

Purpose of this Session:

Although homelessness is a visible problem in the United States and other parts of the world, it is quite misunderstood. Use this TalkSheet to help clear up some of the misconceptions about the issue as well as to challenge your young people to become part of the solution in the name of Jesus.

To Introduce the Topic:

Divide the young people into small groups and tell them they are advertising agencies assigned to create a 30-second public service commercial about the homeless that is going to be on national television during prime time. They need to spotlight the problem of homelessness for TV viewers. Allow enough time for them to make up their skits before they present them to each other.

An alternative would be to have someone unknown to the group impersonate a homeless person (someone who is up-to-date and concerned about the problem) to speak to the group. She or he can give a short talk on the problems a homeless family has—food, shelter, medical care, spiritual problems, life-threatening problems, and so on.

The Discussion:

Item #1: Create a list of feelings. You will be able to generate a larger list than the one found in the activity. Ask the group members why they feel the way they do. Investigate what kind of experiences group members have had with the homeless—caricatures viewed on TV, past work with the homeless, or rumors and the like.

Item #2: Use this activity to identify the different stereotypes people have of the homeless, from the victim down on his luck to the tramp who prefers the lifestyle of the transient. Also talk about what a home provides for people—shelter, protection, dignity, security, and status.

Item #3: Poll the kids on their answers to these statements. If everyone agreed on a particular one, go on to the next. If there is a wide difference of opinion, have a pro and con discussion. Once you have moved through the statements, place the following scale on the chalkboard or on newsprint and have the group members identify where they stand.

|_____|_____|_____|_____|_____|

Homelessness is due to	Homelessness is due to
conditions beyond the	conditions created by
control of the individual	the homeless themselves

Item #4: Point out that homeless people are just like us, created in the image of God. Each of us has the home we do because of the grace of God.

Item #5: In the past there was the notion of the deserving poor and those that did not deserve help. The idea persists today that some individuals who are down on their luck or are very disabled deserve help and that society has a moral obligation to care for them. Ask your kids what Christ might think about this idea. What responsibility do Christians have concerning this enormous social and moral problem?

Item #6: Ask the group how serious Christ was when he delivered this parable. If Christ was serious, how serious will we be in acting on his words?

To Close the Session:

Review the different points made during the discussion. Point out that the problem of homelessness arises from a multitude of conditions existing in our society. There are homeless because of alcoholism, drug addiction, unemployment, chronic mental illness, physical disabilities, AIDS, domestic violence, single parent families, and government policy on affordable housing, to name just the major contributing factors. Some of these people do not want help. They prefer their chosen lifestyles. But most of the homeless want help desperately. Government assistance and homeless shelters are not nearly enough. Emphasize that many homeless people need much more than just shelter. Christ waits for his people to touch the lives of the homeless in his name. Remind the group that Christ was homeless also (Matthew 8:20; Luke 9:58).

Outside Activity:

Ask the group members to create a gratitude list that consists of all the things for which they can be thankful. The list could include the simplest things that we take for granted, like taking a shower.

HERE WE WAR AGAIN

1 Do you know someone who was wounded or killed as a result of a war?

_____ **No**   _____ **Yes**

2 Rank the following social problems from the biggest concern (#1) to the smallest concern (#8).

___ Crime   ___ Hunger and poverty
___ Alcohol and other drug abuse   ___ War or the threat of war
___ Child abuse   ___ Discrimination
___ Family breakdown   ___ Environment

3 What do you think? **A = AGREE   D = DISAGREE**   **A   D**

a. Some video games promote war.   ___   ___
b. War is exciting.   ___   ___
c. There is nothing good about war.   ___   ___
d. It is patriotic to support war.   ___   ___
e. War is avoidable.   ___   ___
f. People should have the right to protest against a war.   ___   ___
g. War is never right.   ___   ___
h. My generation will fight in a war.   ___   ___
i. War promotes peace.   ___   ___
j. Resisting a military draft is a sin.   ___   ___
k. Children should be discouraged from playing with war-type toys.   ___   ___
l. Young people should be willing to die for their country.   ___   ___

4 If your country were to go to war, what would you do? (Check one.)

_____ Never fight, no matter what the reason for the war.
_____ Fight, but only if I thought the war was justified.
_____ Fight, whether or not I thought the war was wrong.

5 Church theologian Augustine articulated seven conditions for a Christian to consider a war justified. His view has come to be known as the Just War. Choose a war in which your country is involved or has been involved. Write it on the line below. From the following Just War list, circle each of the conditions that applies to the war you chose.

Name of the war: _____

a. The reason for the war must be considered just or morally worth the fighting.
b. The only avenue to achieve justice would be through war.
c. If war is entered into, victory must be reasonably assured.
d. The war needs to be declared and waged by a legal authority.
e. War can only be entered into as a last resort.
f. The good achieved must outweigh the bad effects of the war.
g. Only those things that need to be done, should be done to end the war.

6 Choose one of the following Scriptures to rewrite in your own words.

Proverbs 12:20 _____

Matthew 5:9 _____

James 3:17, 18 _____

Date Used: _____

Group: _____

HERE WE WAR AGAIN
Topic: Conventional War

Purpose of this Session:

Christ guaranteed wars and rumors of wars (Matthew 24:6). He also called on Christians to be peacemakers (Matthew 5:9). War is tragic, but it is a fact of life. For the first 300 years of Christian history after the death of Jesus, Christians were pacifists. They refused military service. Today, Christians do not all follow in the steps of those early Christians. Followers of the Prince of Peace have difficulty agreeing on the moral necessity of war. Take time to discuss the issue of war by having a TalkSheet discussion.

To Introduce the Topic:

Break up the teens into small groups. Give each group paper and pens. At a signal, they have one minute to write down as many war movie titles as they possibly can. Give each winning group member a prize, like a toy squirt gun. Tell the group you are going to have a TalkSheet discussion on the topic of conventional war. An additional TalkSheet covering the topic of nuclear war can be found on page 51.

The Discussion:

Item #1: Allow time for the group members to share stories of individuals they may know who have been wounded or killed as a result of war.

Item #2: The problem with war is that we do not consider it a problem until we are at war. Yet the industrial military machine is producing war-making technology at a rapid rate. For peace to be a reality, we must make it a priority.

Item #3: Read the statements aloud and ask for volunteers to express their opinions. Some require more thought and debate than others. Ask the students to explain their answers. Allow dissenting opinions. Not everyone will agree, but all should be allowed their opinions.

Item #4: This personalizes the war issue in a way that forces kids to consider their beliefs and values about war. Offer different potential war scenarios and see how group members respond.

Item #5: Have the group choose one war and put the war on trial. In this war trial, the war is guilty until proven innocent. If the war meets all seven of the Just War conditions, then the war was just. If the war does not meet the criteria, then it was morally wrong to fight the war, according to Augustine's Just War criteria.

Item #6: Divide the teens into small groups and have each interpret one of these verses regarding war and peace. Ask the groups how consistent the verses are with the way their government creates and maintains policy. What can they do to be peacemakers?

To Close the Session:

If one applies the conditions of the Just War theory that has been used throughout the history of Christianity, there are very few wars that can be considered morally justified. And those wars that pass the Just War test have contained elements of war that would flunk. Point out that simply because a government wishes to wage a war, it does not mean that that war is justified. Far too often war has been glorified and equated with patriotism and even Christianity. Yet Christians are called upon to wage peace rather than war. Being a peacemaker can begin wherever you are. Look around you and you will find opportunities to stand up for peace rather than engage in aggression. Conclude the discussion by examining James 4:1-3.

Outside Activity:

Ask groups of students to interview veterans of different wars. Students could find possible interviewees from the church congregation, at a nearby veteran's hospital, at a local military base, at a VFW post, or at a veteran's assistance program. Have the young people compare the viewpoints of veterans from different wars. The group could construct a brief questionnaire so that each veteran is asked the same questions. This makes it easier to compare attitudes about wars.

FAMILY DAZE

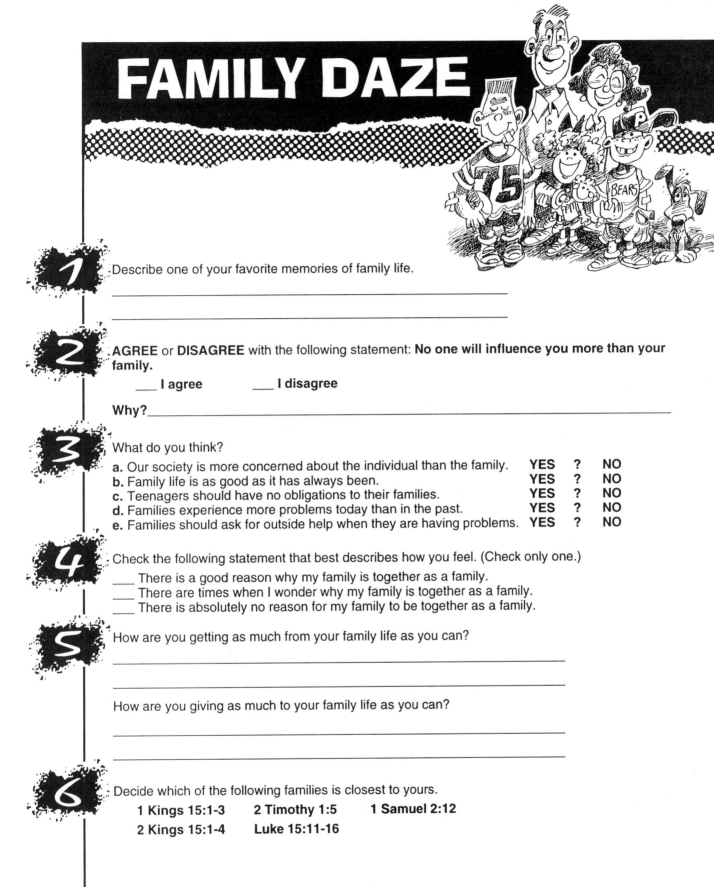

1 Describe one of your favorite memories of family life.

_____

_____

2 AGREE or DISAGREE with the following statement: **No one will influence you more than your family.**

___ **I agree**   ___ **I disagree**

Why?_____

3 What do you think?

a. Our society is more concerned about the individual than the family.   **YES   ?   NO**
b. Family life is as good as it has always been.   **YES   ?   NO**
c. Teenagers should have no obligations to their families.   **YES   ?   NO**
d. Families experience more problems today than in the past.   **YES   ?   NO**
e. Families should ask for outside help when they are having problems.   **YES   ?   NO**

4 Check the following statement that best describes how you feel. (Check only one.)

___ There is a good reason why my family is together as a family.
___ There are times when I wonder why my family is together as a family.
___ There is absolutely no reason for my family to be together as a family.

5 How are you getting as much from your family life as you can?

_____

_____

How are you giving as much to your family life as you can?

_____

_____

6 Decide which of the following families is closest to yours.

1 Kings 15:1-3   2 Timothy 1:5   1 Samuel 2:12

2 Kings 15:1-4   Luke 15:11-16

Date Used: _____

Group: _____

FAMILY DAZE
Topic: Family Life

Purpose of this Session:

Family life needs all the support it can get. Use this TalkSheet to discuss with your group members the important and often overlooked role that family plays in their lives.

To Introduce the Topic:

If you have access to a video camera, here is a great way to introduce the topic of family life. Break the large group into small groups of four to five people. Their assignment is to create a one-minute family home video. Tell the teens that they are to decide on a situation related to the family and develop a skit about it. Suggest titles, such as "Family Fun," "Family Dinner Hour," or "Family Love." Allow a reasonable period of time for planning and rehearsal, and begin filming groups as they are ready. When all the situations have been filmed, gather the whole group together to view the videos. Provide popcorn and soda for added fun.

The Discussion:

Item #1: When asking your young people to share their memories, be sensitive to families that are dysfunctional. At the same time remember that even the most dysfunctional families have some bright memories.

Item #2: The point of this statement is to demonstrate the importance of family. Some kids will not like to admit that their families have influenced them at all. Others are worried about the negative influence their dysfunctional families have had on them. Many young people, however, will have an appreciation of their families' sphere of influence. Ask the young people to identify how their families have influenced them.

Item #3: Have the students share their thoughts and debate the issues that come out of this discussion. The statement, "Teenagers should have no obligations to their families" needs added discussion. Ask the kids what responsibilities they have to their families as they grow older and establish their own particular identities.

Item #4: Let individuals volunteer their perspectives. This activity focuses your young people on the mission of their families. If they do not feel they are getting what they need out of their families, where will they turn? Explain that some kids turn to gang involvement, others to a dysfunctional peer group or an unhealthy male/female relationship. In addition to their families, where else can young people get the love and support they need?

Item #5: This continues where Item #4 left off. Ask the young people to share how they are getting and giving what they need from their families.

Item #6: Each of these passages describes various levels of family devotion to God. Ask the young people what they intend to do with their spiritual heritage—or lack thereof.

To Close the Session:

Summarize the discussion and point out how often family life can seem like a pain and a nuisance. Close, however, with a positive affirmation of family life. Let the group know that you believe in the importance of it. People derive strength, security, love, growth, and development from family relationships. Be sensitive to young people who are living in dysfunctional family situations. Talk about how other families can be role models of family life.

Outside Activity:

For this activity you will need to develop a "Family Tree" handout for each of your group members. This can be a simple design like the one below.

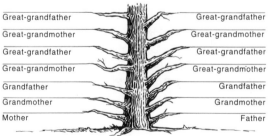

Ask the young people to talk with their parents or grandparents to complete their family trees. They are to go as far back as their great-grandparents if they can. It might be fun for your group members to ask questions about each member. The following are possible questions:

1. Did you have a nickname?
2. Who were you named after?
3. What was your dad like?
4. What games did you play growing up?
5. What did your father do for his career?
6. What did your grandmother look like?

Your group members may have some great questions of their own. Have them report any interesting findings back to the group.

WHAT PLACE WILL CHRIST TAKE?

1 I wish I could go to church or church-related activities . . . (Circle one.)

a. More than once a week
b. Once a week
c. A couple of times a month
d. A couple of times a year
e. Not at all

2 On the line before each of the following statements, write in your response. **YES** or **NO**.

a. _____ I am a Christian, but there are a number of more important things in my life.
b. _____ I want to share my Christianity with others.
c. _____ I work hard at living a Christian life.
d. _____ There are times when I need to hide my Christianity from my friends and acquaintances.
e. _____ My Christian beliefs are not much help in making everyday decisions.
f. _____ The way I look at everyday life is based upon my Christianity.

3 If your Christianity cholesterol was checked, what would be discovered about your Christian life?

_____

_____

4 I am willing to make the following commitment to my Christian life: _____

_____

_____

5 All of the following passages are teachings of Jesus. Synthesize these passages into one or two statements.

Matthew 7:13, 14   **Matthew 7:24-27**   **Matthew 8:18-22**

Matthew 11:28-30   **Luke 14:25-33**

_____

_____

_____

_____

_____

_____

_____

_____

_____

Date Used: _____

Group: _____

WHAT PLACE WILL CHRIST TAKE?
Topic: The Importance of One's Christianity

Purpose of this Session:

Use this TalkSheet opportunity to discuss with your students the importance they place on their Christianity.

To Introduce the Topic:

Replicate on poster paper a one-week page from an appointment book. Divide each day into time segments from 6:00 a.m. to 10:00 p.m. Using suggestions from the group, block out times during each day with activities. A sample day could look like the following:

MONDAY

6:00 a.m.	Get up, eat breakfast, cram for test
7:00 a.m.	Get dressed
8:00 a.m.	Ride bus to school
9:00 a.m.	School
10:00 a.m.	
11:00 a.m.	
NOON	
1:00 p.m.	
2:00 p.m.	
3:00 p.m.	Ride bus home, change for work, eat
4:00 p.m.	Mom drives me to work
5:00 p.m.	Work, soccer practice
6:00 p.m.	
7:00 p.m.	Dinner
8:00 p.m.	Homework

Point out to the group that how we spend our time illustrates what is important to us. Hand out the TalkSheet and tell the teens you are going to discuss how important Christianity is to them.

The Discussion:

Item #1: Ask the young people if church involvement is an indicator of how important one's Christianity is.

Item #2: Items "a," "d," and "e" measure a lower commitment to the Christian life. Items "b," "c," and "f" measure a higher commitment. This short test is not scientifically validated, but it does give you a direction to pursue in the discussion.

Item #3: If your kids do not understand a cholesterol test, explain that adults need this test to monitor their health. Explain that like cholesterol that clogs people's blood vessels, there is also "Christian cholesterol" or junk that keeps us from being committed to Christ. A high Christian cholesterol level is dangerous to your spiritual health.

Item #4: Ask those who are willing to publicly make a commitment to do so, but do not pressure any of your young people to share.

Item #5: Break the kids into groups to do this activity together. Have each group share what it learned.

To Close the Session:

Use the following questions to wrap up the session:

1. How committed do you want to be to your Christian faith?
2. What kind of relationship do you want to have with Jesus Christ?
3. How many things are more important than God?

When God gave the Ten Commandments, he knew that there would be many things that would compete for our attention. That is probably why the first commandment was first (Exodus 20:3). What crowds out God in your life? Whatever it is, it is your "god." You are committed to something! How much of this commitment is directed toward your Christian faith?

Outside Activities:

1. Have your group create a short survey to be given to adults about the importance of one's Christianity. Ask each group member to survey three adults. When the surveys come in, tabulate the results and make some observations about what was learned regarding commitment to the Christian faith.
2. Challenge your group to investigate five Bible characters to see how important their Judaism (Old Testament) or Christianity (New Testament) was to them. They will find that, for the most part, the Bible is a book of failures, not successes. This can be a source of encouragement for your young people, since there is not much difference in people today than in biblical times.

48

BUT I DON'T FEEL CALLED

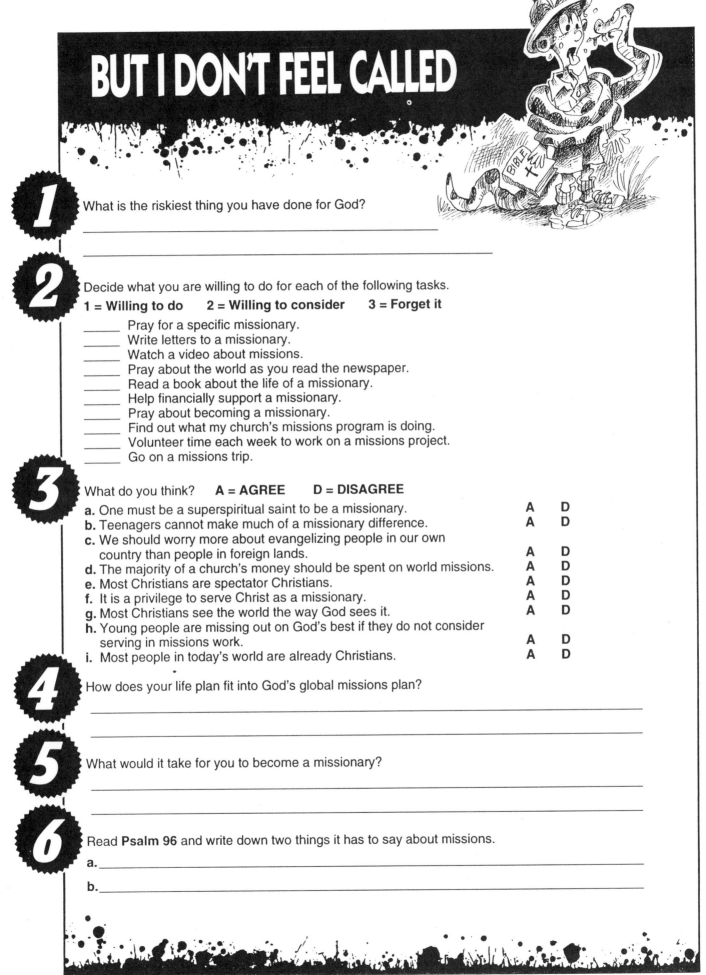

1 What is the riskiest thing you have done for God?

_____

_____

2 Decide what you are willing to do for each of the following tasks.

1 = Willing to do   2 = Willing to consider   3 = Forget it

_____ Pray for a specific missionary.
_____ Write letters to a missionary.
_____ Watch a video about missions.
_____ Pray about the world as you read the newspaper.
_____ Read a book about the life of a missionary.
_____ Help financially support a missionary.
_____ Pray about becoming a missionary.
_____ Find out what my church's missions program is doing.
_____ Volunteer time each week to work on a missions project.
_____ Go on a missions trip.

3 What do you think?   **A = AGREE   D = DISAGREE**

a. One must be a superspiritual saint to be a missionary.   A   D
b. Teenagers cannot make much of a missionary difference.   A   D
c. We should worry more about evangelizing people in our own
   country than people in foreign lands.   A   D
d. The majority of a church's money should be spent on world missions.   A   D
e. Most Christians are spectator Christians.   A   D
f. It is a privilege to serve Christ as a missionary.   A   D
g. Most Christians see the world the way God sees it.   A   D
h. Young people are missing out on God's best if they do not consider
   serving in missions work.   A   D
i. Most people in today's world are already Christians.   A   D

4 How does your life plan fit into God's global missions plan?

_____

_____

5 What would it take for you to become a missionary?

_____

_____

6 Read **Psalm 96** and write down two things it has to say about missions.

a._____

b._____

BUT I DON'T FEEL CALLED
Topic: Missions and Missionaries

Purpose of this Session:

You can expand your group's missions worldview by using this TalkSheet to talk about key issues in the missionary endeavor. Christian young people can and need to understand their part in taking the life-changing message of Jesus Christ to all the world.

To Introduce the Topic:

Create a mock letter from a missionary in a foreign country asking for young people to volunteer their summer to help with missions work to youths. They won't get paid, but the experience will reap eternal rewards. See what kind of response your group makes. Change the scenario with a P.S. that states that if they stay the whole summer, they will get paid well.

Another strategy to introduce the topic is to tell your group you are all going to make up a story about missionaries. Begin by saying, "In a far off country there was a group of missionaries who . . ." then have a young person add the next part of the plot. Let volunteers keep the story going. The only rules are that it should be kept clean and that it should be about missionaries. You are sure to end up with a wild but good introduction to a discussion on missions and missionaries. Many of the myths that persist about missionaries will make their way into the story.

The Discussion:

Item #1: Create a master list of risks. Find out what motivated group members to take risks for God. Ask for examples from the lives of biblical characters of risk-taking for God. Explore how afraid the group is of the concept of missions.

Item #2: Here you have introduced the group to various missions-oriented opportunities. Explore the commitment level of each of the tasks. You may want to wait until you wrap up the discussion before calling the group to commit to any specific tasks.

Item #3: Consider each of the statements and how they apply to winning the world for Christ.

Item #4: Here you can introduce the concept of a World Christian. David Bryant defines World Christians as "day-to-day disciples for whom Christ's global cause has become the integrating, overriding priority for all that He is for them."* World Christians take the Great Commission given by Christ in Matthew 28:18-20 seriously.

Item #5: Challenge the group with the notion that all Christians are called to be missionaries.

Item #6: Examine the passage to see how many truths can be found about missions—party with God, tell all the world about him, the nations are slaves to false gods, the greatness of God, the judgment of God, and so on.

To Close the Session:

Explain to the group that God has a different plan for the world than we do. We have our friends, our families, and our fun times, which are all very important but all too often do not include God and the Gospel. We may like the idea of giving 100 percent of our life to God as long as that does not include going to a foreign land or culture—that is for someone else. Because of our view of the world (a view that does not include the Gospel), we are missing out on the excitement and adventure of being a Christian. Challenge the teens to see the world from God's perspective. Ask them to commit to at least one of the tasks found in Item #2.

Outside Activities:

1. Bring a newspaper to the group. Go through it and examine different local, national, and international events from God's point of view. Ask the group to decide how the Gospel could make a difference in each situation you study.
2. Ridge Burns has put together an exciting book to help your group get into the missions field: *The Complete Student Missions Handbook* (Youth Specialties/Zondervan, 1990). Review his book to see what your group can do.

*David Bryant, *In the Gap: What It Means to Be a World Christian* (Downers Grove, Ill.: InterVarsity Christian Fellowship, 1979), 63.

GROUND ZERO

1 What is the likelihood that nuclear weapons will be used in your lifetime? (Circle one.)
Highly likely   Somewhat likely   Somewhat unlikely   Not likely at all

2 Write out your predictions of what might happen if nuclear weapons are used in the future.

_____

_____

3 As the newly elected president of country X, you have a difficult decision to make. Your country is at war with country Y. Should you use your country's nuclear weapons to end the war sooner and save the lives of your people or continue to use conventional weapons even though you know more of your people will die?

___ **If I were president, I would use nuclear weapons.**
___ **If I were president, I would not use nuclear weapons.**

4 What do you think?   **AGREE   DISAGREE**

a. The world powers need more nuclear weapons to maintain world peace.   _____   _____
b. Nuclear weapons could be used on a limited scale without
   getting out of hand.   _____   _____
c. The average person does not know enough about the threat of nuclear war._____   _____
d. Countries need nuclear weapons for their own self-defense.   _____   _____
e. The threat of nuclear war is one of the biggest problems
   faced by today's world.   _____   _____
f. The Bible has nothing to say about nuclear war.   _____   _____
g. World War III will include the use of nuclear weapons.   _____   _____
h. Nuclear war can be prevented.   _____   _____
i. The church should speak out against the threat of nuclear war.   _____   _____
j. The world is a safer place to live because of nuclear weapons.   _____   _____

5 Answer each of the following questions by placing an **X** on the line at the point best describing you.
a. The possibility of a nuclear war worries me.

  |_____|_____|_____|_____|_____|
  A great deal   **Not at all**

b. The threat of nuclear war affects my everyday life.

  |_____|_____|_____|_____|_____|
  A great deal   **Not at all**

c. The threat of nuclear war affects my future plans.

  |_____|_____|_____|_____|_____|
  A great deal   **Not at all**

6 Study each of the following Scriptures and be prepared to discuss how they apply to nuclear war.
  Romans 12:17-21   James 4:1, 2   1 Peter 3:8-12

Date Used: _____

Group: _____

GROUND ZERO
Topic: Nuclear War

Purpose of this Session:

As long as nuclear weapons exist, the possibility of their use hangs in the air. The anxiety of nuclear war heightens any time there is a world crisis. Study after study has examined the fear, uncertainty, and anxiety that is suppressed in young people about this issue. Feelings of helplessness, denial, and powerlessness are common when this issue is examined with kids as well as adults. Talking about these fears as well as Christ's call to be peacemakers can be the antidote.

To Introduce the Topic:

During the seventh century a man named Hugo Grotius began putting together laws of war to govern how nations fought. These regulations continued to develop and eventually gave us the Declaration of Paris, the Hague Conferences, and the Geneva Conventions. When you watch old war movies, you will often see prisoners mention their rights under the Geneva Convention. These regulations governed how the wounded, the sick, and prisoners were to be treated. Ask your group to hold a Nuclear Wars Convention for the purpose of creating regulations that would govern how nations can conduct nuclear war.

The Discussion:

Item #1: This generation of young people tends to be pessimistic about the future. When one throws the nuclear threat into the future's equation, the outlook of youths tends toward the gloomy. Depending upon the world crisis that is occurring, young people will usually predict the use of at least one or more nuclear weapons during their lifetime. Allow time for the students to vent their feelings.

Item #2: Young people can come up with any number of possibilities. Ask them if any of their potential scenarios are positive ones. How many of them involve massive destruction? Are any of them inevitable? Are there ways that we as Christians can work to avert them? Explore the concept of Armageddon-like thinking: the belief that the end of the world is coming soon and will be hastened by the use of nuclear weapons. For some Christians, it is useless to work toward the prevention of a nuclear holocaust because nuclear war is inevitable. Is this attitude consistent with Christ's call to Christians to be peacemakers?

Item #3: Examine the issue of when, if ever, it would be morally right to use nuclear weapons. President Truman was the first human being to have the power and the weight of this decision upon his shoulders.

Item #4: Open these statements to debate, especially if a difference of opinion exists. Ask for a show of hands on statements that generate extreme differences.

Item #5: Let volunteers share their answers and give reasons for their responses. Then talk about the many ways young people cope with the threat of nuclear war: hedonism, where the attitude is live for today; trust, a feeling that political and military leaders who possess nuclear weapons will use their good judgment; denial, where one does not think about it much; the feeling of indestructibility, "it won't happen to us"; and postmodern progress, the belief that we have learned from the past and will not use nuclear weapons. Discuss with the group how Christ offers hope in the midst of despair.

Item #6: You may wish to divide the group into three smaller ones and assign each a different passage of Scripture. Each group should discuss a passage and report its conclusions.

To Close the Session:

Create a master list of all the points made during the discussion. Then ask the group to distill these points into two or three statements that summarize what has been learned. Close by reading the Sermon on the Mount (Matthew 5:1-12). Contrast Christ's teachings with the way nuclear-capable countries run their foreign policies. Conclude by rereading Matthew 5:9 in which Jesus calls us to be peacemakers.

Outside Activity:

Create a questionnaire including possible statements from Item #4 that group members can use to poll church members. Tabulate the results and discuss them with the group.

I WONDER WHAT THE BIBLE SAYS?

SOLUTION SOURCE

1 What is one problem that faces teenagers that you feel they should

not have to face? _____

2 What do you think?

	REALLY TRUE	SORT OF TRUE	NOT REALLY TRUE
a. When Christians have problems in their lives, they should let God decide what should be done.	____	____	____
b. One's Christian beliefs do not make much difference when looking for solutions to everyday problems.	____	____	____
c. Christians should not think much about problems they face, since it is God's job to tell them what to do.	____	____	____
d. A Christian should work together with God to solve life's problems.	____	____	____
e. When a tough situation is encountered, a young person should figure out what it means on his or her own.	____	____	____
f. God wants to work with us with every problem we face.	____	____	____
g. When a Christian is upset, he or she should ask God to take the anxious feelings away.	____	____	____
h. When faced with a problem, it is best to deal with the feelings one has without leaning on God.	____	____	____
i. God can help a Christian figure out solutions to life's problems.	____	____	____
j. God will somehow work out a Christian's problems for him or her.	____	____	____
k. Rather than tell God our problems, we should take action to work them out.	____	____	____
l. We can work hard to solve life's problems because we know God is working with us.	____	____	____
m. Christians should trust the Lord to give them the answers to their problems.	____	____	____

3 Place an **X** on the line below at the point that best describes you.

|_____|_____|_____|_____|_____|_____|

God solves my problems without my involvement.   **God and I work together to solve my problems.**   **I solve my problems without involving God.**

4 The following are three examples of how believers from the biblical past looked at problems. Choose one to read, then write down your thoughts.

Exodus 4:10-12 _____

_____

Nehemiah 2:2-5 _____

_____

2 Corinthians 1:8-11 _____

_____

SOLUTION SOURCE
Topic: Problem Solving and the Christian

Purpose of this Session:

This TalkSheet offers your young people the opportunity to examine how they approach their problems. Do they solve them themselves, expect God to solve all of them, or cooperate with God in working out their problems?

To Introduce the Topic:

Hand out 3 x 5 cards and pens to the group members. Ask each one to write a problem on one side. Collect the cards, redistribute them blank side up, and ask the teens not to read the problems found on the other side. Then have each kid write a solution to a problem on the blank side. Collect the cards and read the problem and the solution on each card. The results can be hilarious. Announce that this is simply a lead-in to the discussion and that you are not trying to make light of their problems.

The Discussion:

Item #1: Write down each group member's contribution. See if the group can decide upon the top two or three problems.

Item #2: This short, very unscientific quiz can be broken into the following three tracks: a) God solves my problems, b) God and I in partnership solve my problems, or c) I solve my problems alone. Discuss the validity of each of the statements. Ask the students if they have detected a pattern throughout the statements.

Item #3: The young people can score their quizzes using the following scale. Remember this is not a valid test, so do not read too much into their pattern of responses.

a. God solves my problems—Items "a," "c," "g," "j," and "m."

b. God and I in partnership solve my problems—Items "d," "f," "i," and "l."

c. I solve my problems alone—Items "b," "e," "h," and "k."

Kids can have a mixture of responses. The patterns that have the most true responses indicate that their thinking leans in that direction. Have the kids compare their actual quiz responses to the point on the scale that best describes them. Challenge the group to decide which of the three problem solving perspectives is supported by the Bible.

Item #4: Let different individuals share their reflections from each of the three situations. Conclude by reflecting on Romans 8:28.

To Close the Session:

Generally speaking, God is our partner in problem solving. A biblical case can be made for referring all of our problems to God, but most Christians would probably agree that God and his people together work through their issues. He guides and enables us to solve life's problems. Emphasize that God is available to help in solving the problems young people face. But we must ask for his help and be willing to listen when he speaks. That means we must have a relationship with God and God's people so that we can discern what God wants for us. Point out that for a partnership to be formed with God we must *live* our Christian beliefs, not just *use* our Christianity when we encounter a problem.

Outside Activity:

Take a serious look at the problems written for the introductory activity. You can read each of the problems and ask the group to brainstorm solutions that include how God can help. Challenge the group to provide biblical passages as encouragement.

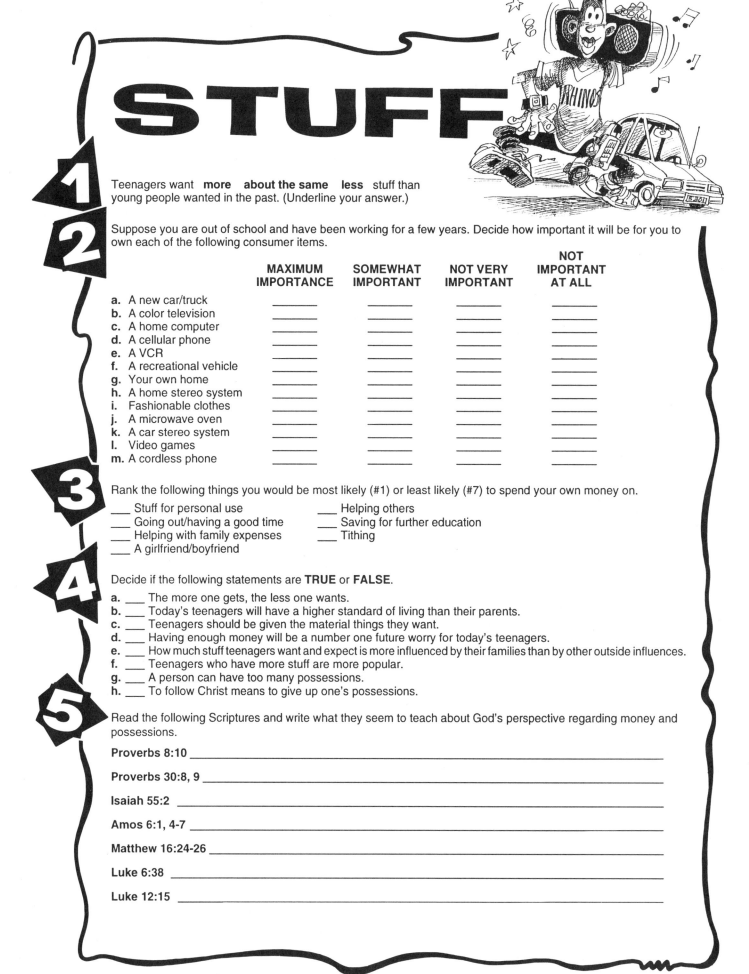

STUFF

1 Teenagers want **more** **about the same** **less** stuff than young people wanted in the past. (Underline your answer.)

2 Suppose you are out of school and have been working for a few years. Decide how important it will be for you to own each of the following consumer items.

	MAXIMUM IMPORTANCE	SOMEWHAT IMPORTANT	NOT VERY IMPORTANT	NOT IMPORTANT AT ALL
a. A new car/truck	_____	_____	_____	_____
b. A color television	_____	_____	_____	_____
c. A home computer	_____	_____	_____	_____
d. A cellular phone	_____	_____	_____	_____
e. A VCR	_____	_____	_____	_____
f. A recreational vehicle	_____	_____	_____	_____
g. Your own home	_____	_____	_____	_____
h. A home stereo system	_____	_____	_____	_____
i. Fashionable clothes	_____	_____	_____	_____
j. A microwave oven	_____	_____	_____	_____
k. A car stereo system	_____	_____	_____	_____
l. Video games	_____	_____	_____	_____
m. A cordless phone	_____	_____	_____	_____

3 Rank the following things you would be most likely (#1) or least likely (#7) to spend your own money on.

___ Stuff for personal use   ___ Helping others
___ Going out/having a good time   ___ Saving for further education
___ Helping with family expenses   ___ Tithing
___ A girlfriend/boyfriend

4 Decide if the following statements are **TRUE** or **FALSE**.

a. ___ The more one gets, the less one wants.
b. ___ Today's teenagers will have a higher standard of living than their parents.
c. ___ Teenagers should be given the material things they want.
d. ___ Having enough money will be a number one future worry for today's teenagers.
e. ___ How much stuff teenagers want and expect is more influenced by their families than by other outside influences.
f. ___ Teenagers who have more stuff are more popular.
g. ___ A person can have too many possessions.
h. ___ To follow Christ means to give up one's possessions.

5 Read the following Scriptures and write what they seem to teach about God's perspective regarding money and possessions.

Proverbs 8:10 _____

Proverbs 30:8, 9 _____

Isaiah 55:2 _____

Amos 6:1, 4-7 _____

Matthew 16:24-26 _____

Luke 6:38 _____

Luke 12:15 _____

STUFF

Topic: The Consumption Expectations of Teenagers

Purpose of this Session:

The consumption aspirations and patterns of our general society have adversely affected young people. The mass media seem to have supplanted the traditional purveyor of values, the family, in influencing the consumption expectations of kids. Poor, middle-class, and rich kids alike report high levels of present and future expectations of material goods. But are these consumption patterns Christian? This TalkSheet explores the topic of possessions and consumption expectations held by young people.

To Introduce the Topic:

Give each person a piece of paper and a pen. Have the teens make a list of all the stuff they are wearing, including what is in their wallets, pockets, and purses. You can also have them include things like glasses, contact lenses, and braces. Next to each item they should write down an estimate of how much it costs. They can then calculate a total amount of the worth of what they are wearing. Use yourself as an example to explain what needs to be done. Add up the individual totals and you may be surprised at the amount of money that has been spent on the group. Often this amount will be more than the annual incomes of families in Third World countries.

The Discussion:

Item #1: This item gives an historical perspective regarding possessions. In the past young people did not have as much because there was not as much to have. Today, a person could fill a warehouse full of consumer goods.

Item #2: Here you will get at the kids' consumption expectations. Ask them why they plan to own the things they identified. How can the things they want get in the way of their relationship with God? How much stuff is enough?

Item #3: This activity identifies the priorities of your group members. Have the kids guess how Jesus might rank these, and compare the two lists.

Item #4: Ask the group members to share their choices and their reasons why.

Item #5: In the Bible, Christ had much to say about money and possessions because they are so dangerous. Some of the Bible passages are very straightforward; other passages are paradoxical. Examine them and decide which make the most sense and which seem to be paradoxes. Come to some conclusions about God's view of possessions and money. Ask the group to decide which, if any, of these passages are lived out by the average person in our society.

To Close the Session:

Using the introductory exercise, remind the group of the activity, and challenge the kids to convince a teenager from an average Third World country that your youth group members are not rich.

In the past people had less stuff than we do now. Today we add more storage space to our lives with closet space savers, storage sheds, and rental storage space. We consume more and more. But God's kingdom turns things around. God says you must give in order to get; you must lose your life to save it. Christ repeatedly warned his disciples about the dangers of possessions. They get in the way of living life. Christ enjoyed life as he served God. Luke 7:34 suggests that the Pharisees felt maybe he was enjoying it too much. It was not enjoyment or happiness that Jesus warned us against but the belief that our possessions will provide that happiness. It is our attitudes toward stuff that get us into trouble. Consider the parable of the sower found in Matthew 13 (see especially verse 22).

Outside Activity:

Challenge the students to sacrificially give up some of their stuff to people less fortunate than themselves. This can be a group project where a need is identified, such as a local homeless shelter or a battered women's shelter. The group members then choose to give some of their personal possessions to meet the identified need.

PEER POWER

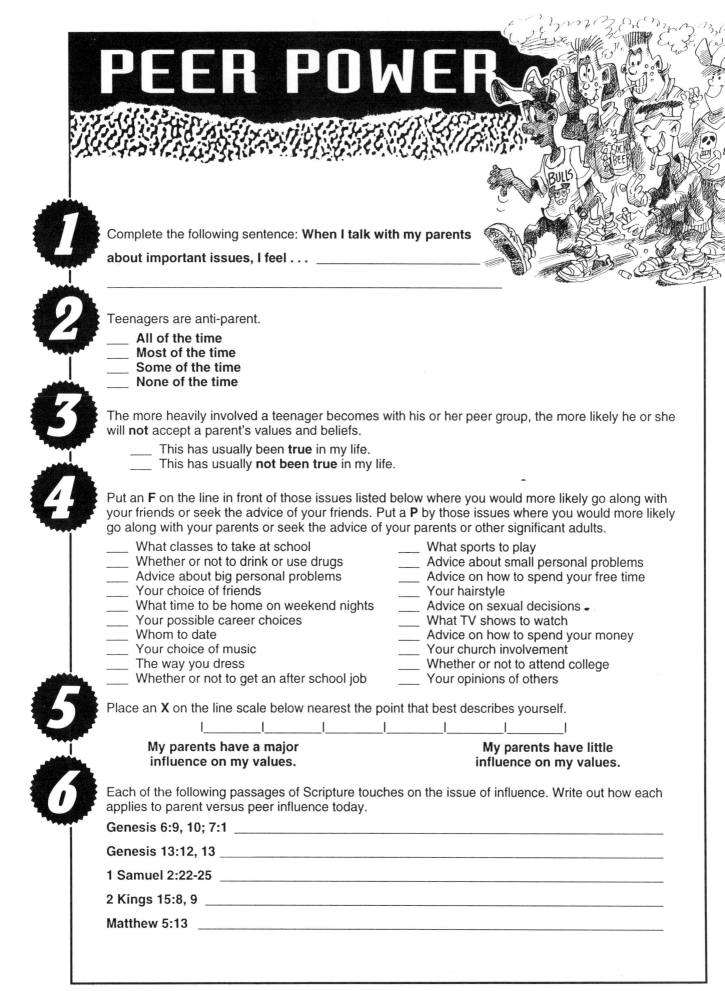

1 Complete the following sentence: **When I talk with my parents about important issues, I feel . . .** _____

_____

2 Teenagers are anti-parent.

___ **All of the time**
___ **Most of the time**
___ **Some of the time**
___ **None of the time**

3 The more heavily involved a teenager becomes with his or her peer group, the more likely he or she will **not** accept a parent's values and beliefs.

___ This has usually been **true** in my life.
___ This has usually **not been true** in my life.

4 Put an **F** on the line in front of those issues listed below where you would more likely go along with your friends or seek the advice of your friends. Put a **P** by those issues where you would more likely go along with your parents or seek the advice of your parents or other significant adults.

___ What classes to take at school
___ Whether or not to drink or use drugs
___ Advice about big personal problems
___ Your choice of friends
___ What time to be home on weekend nights
___ Your possible career choices
___ Whom to date
___ Your choice of music
___ The way you dress
___ Whether or not to get an after school job

___ What sports to play
___ Advice about small personal problems
___ Advice on how to spend your free time
___ Your hairstyle
___ Advice on sexual decisions
___ What TV shows to watch
___ Advice on how to spend your money
___ Your church involvement
___ Whether or not to attend college
___ Your opinions of others

5 Place an **X** on the line scale below nearest the point that best describes yourself.

|_____|_____|_____|_____|_____|_____|

My parents have a major influence on my values.　　　　**My parents have little influence on my values.**

6 Each of the following passages of Scripture touches on the issue of influence. Write out how each applies to parent versus peer influence today.

Genesis 6:9, 10; 7:1 _____

Genesis 13:12, 13 _____

1 Samuel 2:22-25 _____

2 Kings 15:8, 9 _____

Matthew 5:13 _____

Date Used: _____

Group: _____

PEER POWER
Topic: The Influence of Parents and Peers

Purpose of this Session:

Parents of teenagers lie in bed worrying about a number of things. Peer group influence is at the top of many lists. One of your responsibilities as a youth leader is to affirm the role parents play in the lives of young people while at the same time helping kids live in the world of their peers. Use this TalkSheet to talk about the role of parents and peers in the lives of the young people in your group.

To Introduce the Topic:

For this introductory activity you will need to make a number of street signs from 8 1/2 x 11 sheets of paper. Place directional arrows on them and write out statements of direction or influence that a parent or a peer might say to a kid. Below are some sample statements. Tape these signs around the room. Ask the group to read the signs and help you place them under one of two categories: "Something a parent would most likely say" or "Something a peer would most likely say." Then explain to the teens that these signs are examples of ways parents and peers influence them.

"You can't always get what you want."
"But everybody is doing it."
"You don't do everything your parents tell you, do you?"
"If I've told you once, I've told you a thousand times . . ."
"Just this once . . ."
"You will have to earn my trust."

"Your mom will never find out."
"Be back by . . ."
"I dare you to . . ."
"I'm glad my parents aren't like that."
"When I was your age . . ."

The Discussion:

Item #1: Keep this on a feeling level. Do kids feel comfortable, uncomfortable, anxious, excited, nervous, angry, or happy? Ask the students to give examples that illustrate why they feel the way they do.

Item #2: Let young people respond to the statement. Have the group reach a consensus. Reverse the question: Are parents anti-teenager? How about adults in general? Does this affect how young people accept adult values and beliefs?

Item #3: Many in your group will say this has not been true in their lives. Most kids do not believe that peer pressure affects their deeper selves. They feel they are their own persons and make up their own minds. If most in your group report that this is not true, then discuss how they are like their parents. What values of their parents have they accepted? How do they ensure they will not be influenced negatively? Point out that some young people are adversely influenced by their parents. What should those young people do?

Item #4: After kids share some of their responses, ask the group to summarize a basic statement about this issue. For example, the more important and far-ranging the issue, the more likely the young person will be influenced by parents. Or, the older one gets the more likely she or he is to listen to peers over parents.

Item #5: Ask questions like, "Should parents have a major influence on values?" "Why do parents want to influence your values?" "If parents are not the ones influencing your values, who is?"

Item #6: Let the young people share what they discovered. Focus on Matthew 5:13 and ask how Christian young people can influence (salt) both their parents and their peers. This introduces a more proactive slant to the discussion so that your group members become active influencers rather than passive objects of influence.

To Close the Session:

Explain to the students that they live in two worlds. On the one hand is the family with all these expectations, demands, hopes, and plans for them. On the other is the peer group that also has expectations, demands, hopes, and plans for them. Balancing these two worlds can sometimes seem impossible, but that is where their Christian faith can help. Explain that God is not against their friends or their parents. He has offered some guidelines in the Bible, not as killjoy principles, but as a road map to guide them. Read **Proverbs 1:8-19** and tell the group that this is only one guideline that must be balanced with others. Generally speaking, they can rely on their parents for the important things in life, and they must weigh carefully what their friends say. At other times and in some family situations, parents' advice is shakier than that of friends. God's advice and the help of trustworthy Christians are always available. Emphasize the normalcy of being comfortable with peers—most people *are* more open with their peers (including their own parents with their own peers).

Outside Activity:

During your TalkSheet discussion, a number of situations will be brought up as illustrations. Write four or five of these down and ask the group to take them home. Have them ask for their parents' input and bring it back to the group to compare notes. The kids will be amazed at the similarity in the parental responses.

WHERE DO WE GO FROM HERE?

1 When you hear about the afterlife, what is the first thing you think about?

_____

_____

2 What do you think? **A = AGREE**   **NS = NOT SURE**   **D = DISAGREE**

	A	NS	D
a. People who live good lives will go to heaven.	A	NS	D
b. Reincarnation makes as much sense as a heaven.	A	NS	D
c. There is no good reason to believe there is a hell.	A	NS	D
d. Christians talk more about hell than they do about heaven.	A	NS	D
e. Hell will not be as bad a place as preachers make it out to be.	A	NS	D
f. The average young person believes in a heaven **more** than a hell.	A	NS	D
g. Talking about hell will scare people into wanting to know more about how to get to heaven.	A	NS	D
h. Christians should be more worried about the here and now than about the afterlife.	A	NS	D
i. If there is a heaven, there must be a hell.	A	NS	D
j. The belief in heaven keeps people from seeking happiness on earth.	A	NS	D

3 Will life in heaven be **more real** or **less real** than life on earth? Why? _____

_____

_____

4 How can your views about heaven and hell affect the way you live your life? ____ _____

_____

_____

5 Read the following Scriptures and write what you think each passage has to say about heaven and/or hell.

Matthew 25:46 _____

_____

Luke 16:24-26 _____

_____

1 Corinthians 1:18 _____

_____

Philippians 1:23, 24 _____

_____

2 Peter 2:4-9 _____

_____

WHERE DO WE GO FROM HERE?
Topic: Heaven and Hell

Purpose of this Session:

Scripture provides only glimpses of what heaven and hell will be like. But the Bible clearly teaches that both exist. There has been a resurgence of interest in the afterlife because of the new age emphasis on reincarnation. Even people who do not hold to religious beliefs express interest in the afterlife. Talk shows have guests who claim to have died and seen the afterlife. Magazines write about people who claim they have lived before and will do so again. Opinion polls report people's views regarding the afterlife. This TalkSheet encourages a group examination of both heaven and hell.

To Introduce the Topic:

Break into groups of three to four and assign each group the task of creating either a music video about heaven or a music video about hell. Each group must decide what visual images will appear, who the stars will be, and what music will be featured on the heaven or hell music videos.

Another introductory activity would be to take an imaginary skateboard trip through heaven and hell. Begin in hell and then move through heaven. Ask the kids to describe what they might see on their trip.

The Discussion:

Item #1: Allow group members to share their thoughts about the afterlife. Pay particular attention to how your group has been influenced by secular views—there is no hell, the afterlife will be boring, and reincarnation really happens.

Item #2: Take a poll on each of the statements. If there is total agreement on one, go to the next. If there is a difference of opinion, encourage a debate on their ideas. You may wish to study these ahead of time in order to make well-founded comments of your own. Item "j" warrants extra discussion. It was Karl Marx, the founder of communism, who believed religion and the concept of a heaven and a hell kept the average person oppressed. According to Marx, dwelling on heaven and a reward in the afterlife kept people from seeking justice on earth. Ask the students if they feel Marx was right or wrong. Does believing in heaven and hell keep Christians from serving God and others on earth?

Item #3: This question can be a mind-stopper for many. People often think of heaven as blissful nothingness where we sit on clouds and talk about God. Yet the Bible speaks of real streets and tasks that serve God. Heaven is a very real place. Paul spoke of seeing things as a poor reflection in a mirror, but in heaven we shall see things as they really are (1 Corinthians 13:12).

Item #4: You can use 2 Peter 3:11-13 as a discussion text.

Item #5: The Bible does not tell us everything we would like to know about heaven and hell, but it does give us glimpses of both. Have the group members share what they learned about heaven and hell and their attitudes toward them.

To Close the Session:

We cannot talk about heaven without talking about hell and vice versa. The Bible tells us that both are real and both are required. What God has given us is a choice. When kids ask why a loving God would condemn anyone to hell, they are asking the wrong question. The real question is why would anyone want to reject God's love? God wants everyone to experience eternal life with him (John 5:24; 2 Peter 3:9).

Outside Activity:

Ask the students to interview senior adults in your church about their feelings toward heaven and hell. Have them compare their views with the views expressed by their elders.

TUNED IN

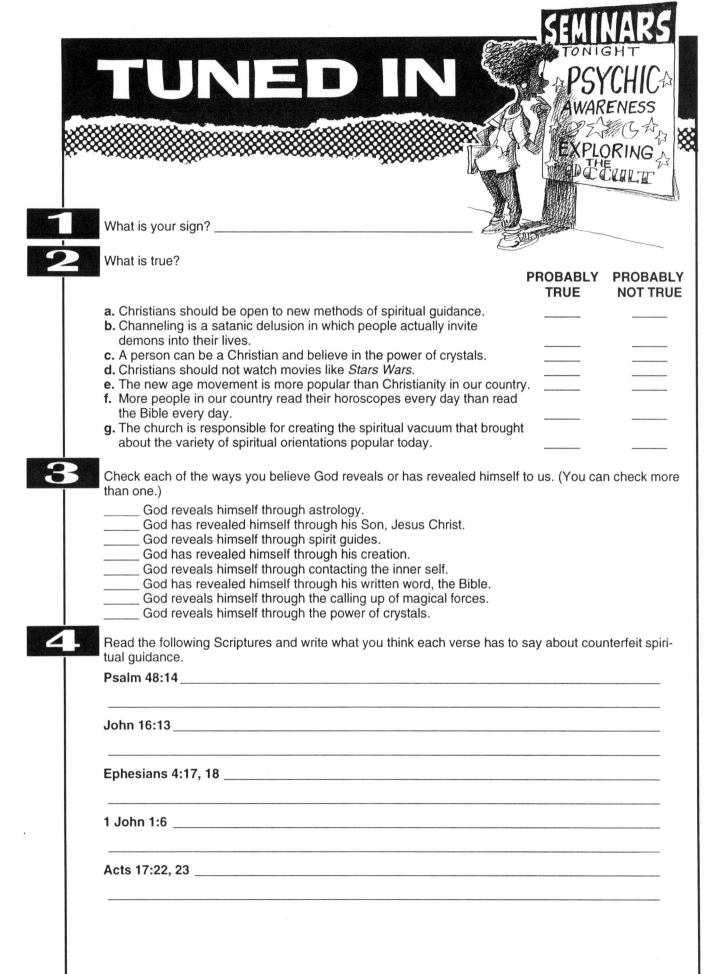

1 What is your sign? _____

2 What is true?

	PROBABLY TRUE	PROBABLY NOT TRUE
a. Christians should be open to new methods of spiritual guidance.	_____	_____
b. Channeling is a satanic delusion in which people actually invite demons into their lives.	_____	_____
c. A person can be a Christian and believe in the power of crystals.	_____	_____
d. Christians should not watch movies like *Stars Wars*.	_____	_____
e. The new age movement is more popular than Christianity in our country.	_____	_____
f. More people in our country read their horoscopes every day than read the Bible every day.	_____	_____
g. The church is responsible for creating the spiritual vacuum that brought about the variety of spiritual orientations popular today.	_____	_____

3 Check each of the ways you believe God reveals or has revealed himself to us. (You can check more than one.)

_____ God reveals himself through astrology.
_____ God has revealed himself through his Son, Jesus Christ.
_____ God reveals himself through spirit guides.
_____ God has revealed himself through his creation.
_____ God reveals himself through contacting the inner self.
_____ God has revealed himself through his written word, the Bible.
_____ God reveals himself through the calling up of magical forces.
_____ God reveals himself through the power of crystals.

4 Read the following Scriptures and write what you think each verse has to say about counterfeit spiritual guidance.

Psalm 48:14 _____

_____

John 16:13 _____

_____

Ephesians 4:17, 18 _____

_____

1 John 1:6 _____

_____

Acts 17:22, 23 _____

_____

Date Used: _____

Group: _____

TUNED IN
Topic: Counterfeit Spiritual Guidance

Purpose of this Session:

There has been a revival of counterfeit spiritual forces that are having an impact on our culture in profound ways. One significant impact is upon young people. East now meets West on the school campus. Meditation, crystals, astrology, Indian religions, witchcraft, and spirit guides are more common than adults realize. Take this opportunity to talk about these spiritual counterfeits with your group through a TalkSheet discussion.

To Introduce the Topic:

Have a radio in front of you as you begin this activity. Demonstrate that your radio can provide you with entertainment, news, and information by tuning into different frequencies. When you tune into different stations, you receive different broadcasts. If you are not familiar with the stations, you have to search for program formats you like. If you are not sure what you want to listen to, you could tune into many kinds of programs. Some would be better than others. Ask the group how the radio is like spiritual guidance. Tell them that there is an abundance of spiritual counterfeits trying to get the attention of young people, and many teens are tuning into these counterfeits. Then pass out the TalkSheets and begin your discussion on spiritual guidance.

The Discussion:

Item #1: This activity is not designed to excite or entice your kids into astrology. Rather it is intended to illustrate how familiar we are with it. Ask the group how astrology is affecting people today. Point out the 1-900 astrology telephone numbers and the astrology guides in most newspapers.

Item #2: Expect debate and questions about each of these statements. Explain that Item "a" is not talking about the traditional spiritual disciplines but about new methods like Eastern meditation, crystals, astrology, medicine wheels, and the like. Item "b" is interesting because more young people are experimenting with channeling and spirit guides at parties and sleep overs. They learn about them from friends and movies. Item "d" requires extra discussion because there are so many movies with a new age or satanic bent. *Star Wars* is an example of a movie based upon Eastern religious thought. Ask the kids which movies are deceptive and dangerous and which are not.

Item #3: God reveals himself in the following ways: He has revealed himself through his Son, Jesus Christ; he has revealed himself through his written word, the Bible; and he has revealed himself through his creation.

Item #4: Ask the students to share their thoughts on what they learned.

To Close the Session:

The best defense against counterfeit spiritual guidance is a good offense. Emphasize to the kids that the more they know about God's truth, the less likely they are to be duped by spiritual counterfeits. Discuss the idea that there are two ways to be fooled: one is to believe what isn't so, and the other is to refuse to believe what is. Point out to the group that many people are fooled simply because they do not want to believe in God and his Son, Jesus Christ. Or they believe but do little else to grow in their faith. They fall for the counterfeits because they know very little about what is real. Many other people are fooled and manipulated by counterfeit religions and beliefs because they will believe anything without investigating its validity. Then there are those who cannot be deceived because they are committed to what is real, what is truth. Ask the kids which category they fall into. Conclude by reading Deuteronomy 18:9-15.

Outside Activity:

You can obtain additional information for your group to study regarding the issues raised by writing to Spiritual Counterfeit Projects, P.O. Box 4308, Berkeley, CA 94704.

ALCOHOL AND OTHER DRUGS

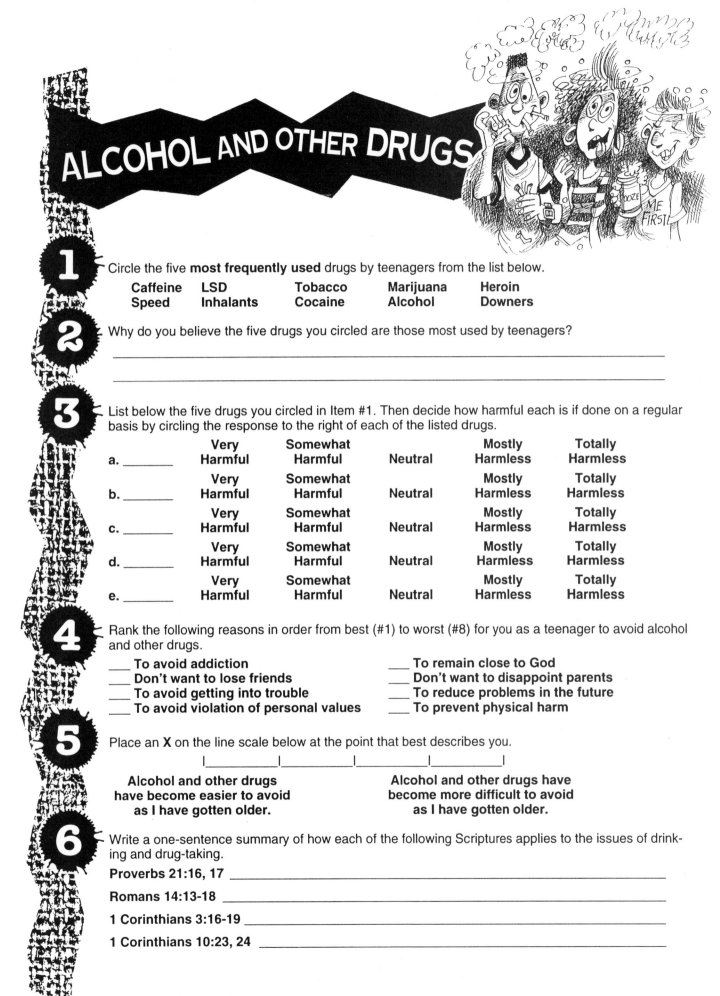

1 Circle the five **most frequently used** drugs by teenagers from the list below.

Caffeine	LSD	Tobacco	Marijuana	Heroin
Speed	Inhalants	Cocaine	Alcohol	Downers

2 Why do you believe the five drugs you circled are those most used by teenagers?

_____

_____

3 List below the five drugs you circled in Item #1. Then decide how harmful each is if done on a regular basis by circling the response to the right of each of the listed drugs.

	Very Harmful	Somewhat Harmful	Neutral	Mostly Harmless	Totally Harmless
a. _____	Very Harmful	Somewhat Harmful	Neutral	Mostly Harmless	Totally Harmless
b. _____	Very Harmful	Somewhat Harmful	Neutral	Mostly Harmless	Totally Harmless
c. _____	Very Harmful	Somewhat Harmful	Neutral	Mostly Harmless	Totally Harmless
d. _____	Very Harmful	Somewhat Harmful	Neutral	Mostly Harmless	Totally Harmless
e. _____	Very Harmful	Somewhat Harmful	Neutral	Mostly Harmless	Totally Harmless

4 Rank the following reasons in order from best (#1) to worst (#8) for you as a teenager to avoid alcohol and other drugs.

___ **To avoid addiction**   ___ **To remain close to God**
___ **Don't want to lose friends**   ___ **Don't want to disappoint parents**
___ **To avoid getting into trouble**   ___ **To reduce problems in the future**
___ **To avoid violation of personal values**   ___ **To prevent physical harm**

5 Place an **X** on the line scale below at the point that best describes you.

|_____|_____|_____|_____|

Alcohol and other drugs   **Alcohol and other drugs have**
have become easier to avoid   **become more difficult to avoid**
as I have gotten older.   **as I have gotten older.**

6 Write a one-sentence summary of how each of the following Scriptures applies to the issues of drinking and drug-taking.

Proverbs 21:16, 17 _____

Romans 14:13-18 _____

1 Corinthians 3:16-19 _____

1 Corinthians 10:23, 24 _____

ALCOHOL AND OTHER DRUGS
Topic: Alcohol and Drug Use

Purpose of this Session:

Alcohol and other drug use is an issue that remains problematic in society. The title of this TalkSheet pur-posefully includes alcohol with drugs so that young people will understand that there is no difference. This is not to suggest that adults should not drink in moderation. But those adults as well as young people need to understand that when they drink they are consuming a legal drug. Take the opportunity to talk with your young people about drugs and how they can avoid them.

To Introduce the Topic:

Ask an adult Christian and a teenager in recovery from addiction to discuss chemical dependency and recov-ery. The recovering person can answer questions as well. Let the guest speaker know that you do not want the issue of alcohol and drug use to be glamorized and glorified. Often speakers tell funny stories about when they were using, then only briefly talk about their addictions and struggles with recovery.

The Discussion:

Item #1: Let the young people add drugs to the list using the slang of the day. Generally speaking, the three most frequently used drugs are caffeine, tobacco, and alcohol. Point out that these three are addictive drugs even though they are legal. Alcohol is a poison and a drug in liquid form. The other two choices will depend upon your community.

Item #2: Create a master list of reasons why these drugs are used by teenagers.

Item #3: Let the young people debate the harmfulness of each of these drugs. Like adults, kids using drugs tend to discount their harmfulness. For example, caffeine's dangers have been documented, yet we who drink sodas with caffeine tend to discount this harmfulness. The same is true for coffee, beer, or even marijuana.

Item #4: Here the group can focus on good reasons to avoid use. Reach a group consensus on the best reasons to avoid use.

Item #5: Role-play situations that the young people identify as problematic. Practice in alcohol/drug use refusal can help kids when they face difficult situations.

Item #6: Let group members share their various perspectives on the passages. Focus on one or two of the Scriptures of interest to the group.

To Close the Session:

Do not lecture the group. Instead ask several group members to summarize what has been discussed and to offer closing comments. You can then share your personal convictions regarding this issue.

Outside Activity:

Ask an adult Christian and a teenager in recovery from chemical dependency to discuss chemical depen-dency and recovery. The recovering person can answer questions as well. Explain to the guest speakers that alcohol and drug use should not be glamorized or glorified (sometimes speakers tell funny stories of when they were using, then only briefly talk about their addictions and struggles with recovery).

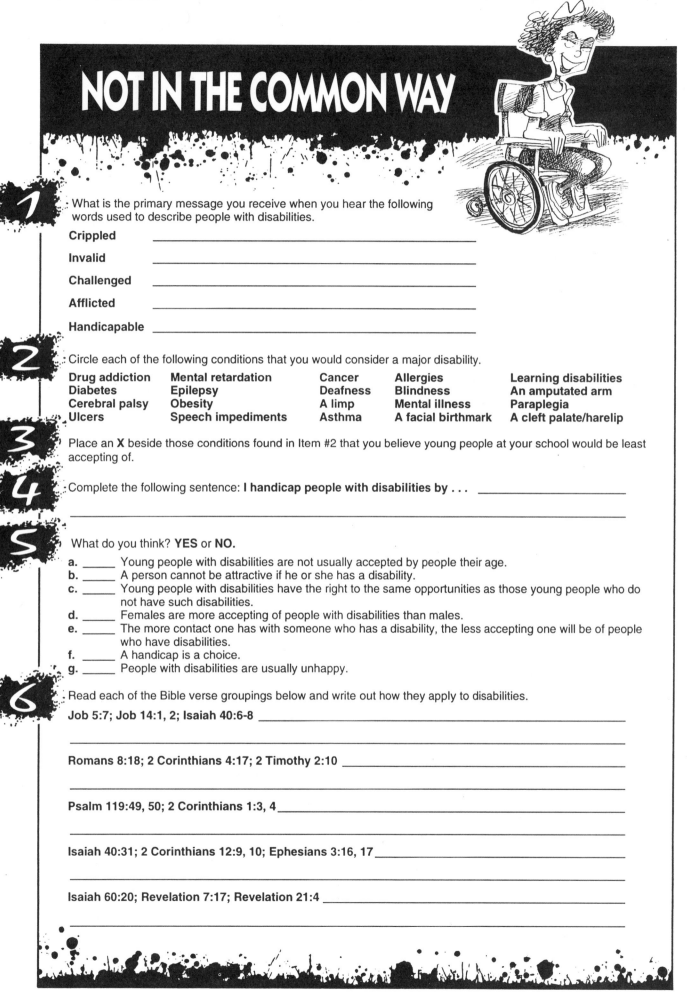

NOT IN THE COMMON WAY

1 What is the primary message you receive when you hear the following words used to describe people with disabilities.

Crippled _____

Invalid _____

Challenged _____

Afflicted _____

Handicapable _____

2 Circle each of the following conditions that you would consider a major disability.

Drug addiction	**Mental retardation**	**Cancer**	**Allergies**	**Learning disabilities**
Diabetes	**Epilepsy**	**Deafness**	**Blindness**	**An amputated arm**
Cerebral palsy	**Obesity**	**A limp**	**Mental illness**	**Paraplegia**
Ulcers	**Speech impediments**	**Asthma**	**A facial birthmark**	**A cleft palate/harelip**

3 Place an **X** beside those conditions found in Item #2 that you believe young people at your school would be least accepting of.

4 Complete the following sentence: **I handicap people with disabilities by . . .** _____

_____

5 What do you think? **YES** or **NO**.

a. _____ Young people with disabilities are not usually accepted by people their age.

b. _____ A person cannot be attractive if he or she has a disability.

c. _____ Young people with disabilities have the right to the same opportunities as those young people who do not have such disabilities.

d. _____ Females are more accepting of people with disabilities than males.

e. _____ The more contact one has with someone who has a disability, the less accepting one will be of people who have disabilities.

f. _____ A handicap is a choice.

g. _____ People with disabilities are usually unhappy.

6 Read each of the Bible verse groupings below and write out how they apply to disabilities.

Job 5:7; Job 14:1, 2; Isaiah 40:6-8 _____

_____

Romans 8:18; 2 Corinthians 4:17; 2 Timothy 2:10 _____

_____

Psalm 119:49, 50; 2 Corinthians 1:3, 4 _____

_____

Isaiah 40:31; 2 Corinthians 12:9, 10; Ephesians 3:16, 17 _____

_____

Isaiah 60:20; Revelation 7:17; Revelation 21:4 _____

_____

Date Used:_____

Group:_____

NOT IN THE COMMON WAY
Topic: Disabilities

Purpose of this Session:
Young people are often ignorant of the difficulties encountered by people who have disabilities. This TalkSheet offers the opportunity to discuss what it means to have a disability and reviews a Christian response.

To Introduce the Topic:
Illustrate various disabilities by using one or more of the following simulated exercises.

1. Have half the kids walk around the building and grounds blindfolded with the other half acting as their guides. After five minutes, switch roles. Keep safety in mind while doing this.
2. Check out a book from the library that teaches sign language and teach the group several common words.
3. Have the kids take dictation from you as you tell a story. They must use the opposite hand than they normally use for writing. Keep the story moving. This mildly simulates what it is like to have cerebral palsy.

The Discussion:
Item #1: Other words unfortunately sometimes used to describe those with disabilities are *the infirmed, shut-ins, defective, handicapped, deformed,* and *disabled.* Point out to the group that we need to use the term "people with disabilities" rather than "the disabled," "the handicapped," or "the crippled." *Handicapable* is a word that more positively affirms anyone who has a disability. Discuss the myth that disability equals inability, which is simply not true.

Item #2: Discuss why people view their choices as major disabilities. Define with the group what a major disability really is. One person's handicap is another's advantage.

Item #3: Brainstorm how Christians can influence others to be more accepting of those with disabilities.

Item #4: Explain that a disability is the condition and a handicap is something that keeps a person from doing something. Ask the group to identify how attitudes and actions handicap people with disabilities. Have the kids list the ways people with disabilities are like everyone else.

Item #5: Ask for a vote of yes or no on each of the statements. Item "c" deserves extra discussion. Decide how young people with disabilities are discriminated against. Item "f" can be quite controversial. Connect this statement with Item #4. Item "g" is one of the many myths about people with disabilities; they are no more or less happy than the average person.

Item #6: Break the kids into groups, each taking a grouping of Scriptures to work on.

To Close the Session:
The following points can help you in wrapping up the session.

1. People with disabilities are people. They are not patients or sick.
2. People with disabilities need to be treated with dignity and respect. They too often are treated like objects. We talk for them or at them, not with them. We do not need to do for them what they can do for themselves.
3. All of us have disabilities that limit us in one or more ways. Some of us have more severe disabilities than others.
4. Disabilities like mental retardation are not contagious. You do not catch them like the flu.
5. We need to be sensitive to the ways we discriminate against those with disabilities. When we park in a handicapped parking spot and rationalize that we will just be a minute, we are discriminating against people with disabilities.
6. Disability does not equal inability.
7. Christ died for all people.
8. Christ has called all Christians to a higher calling of compassion and redemption.

THE DIVORCE DOCTOR

1 When you think of divorce, what usually pops into your mind?

_____

_____

2 Underline each of the following that you believe most teenagers experience when their parents are getting divorced or have divorced.

Crazy feelings   **Low self-esteem**   **Hassles with living with one parent**
Psychiatric problems   **Parent playing the dating game**   **Post-divorce money problems**
Abandonment   **Weird holidays**   **Parent visitation problems**
Problems with drugs   **Anger toward God**   **Few adjustment problems**
Listening to one parent gripe about the other

3 For each of the following situations, give your advice.

SITUATION	ADVICE

a. "My dad left my mom and moved in with his girlfriend. He expects me   _____

to treat this new lady like she is someone special."   _____

b. "I want to live with my dad. When my parents divorced, my mom   _____

moved my little sister and me to another state. But we are not getting   _____

along and it has been two years."   _____

c. "I feel like my dad has dumped me. Since my parents' divorce, I hardly   _____

ever see him. The first year he came around quite often. But not now. I   _____

can't figure out what I have done wrong. My mom says he'll never change."   _____

d. "My mom and dad expect me to be their messenger. My dad says to   _____

tell my mother such and such and my mom does the same. I'm tired of   _____

being in the middle but I don't know what to do!"   _____

e. "I hate it that my mom is dating. She brings home the weirdest guys."   _____

4 What do you think?   **M = THAT'S ME**   **N = THAT'S NOT ME**

a. I will probably get divorced someday.   **M**   **N**
b. I could never forgive my parents for getting divorced.   **M**   **N**
c. It is not that big a deal to handle your parents' divorce.   **M**   **N**
d. I feel I could have stopped or could stop my parents from divorcing.   **M**   **N**
e. I would like my marriage to be like that of my parents.   **M**   **N**
f. Talking about a parents' divorce to people who care helps ease the pain of divorce. **M**   **N**

5 Rewrite **Psalm 23** to apply to teenagers recovering from their parents' divorce.

_____

_____

_____

_____

Date Used: _____

Group: _____

THE DIVORCE DOCTOR
Topic: Divorce

Purpose of this Session:

This TalkSheet is not about the rightness or wrongness of divorce. Teens are not responsible for their parents' marital dissolution, but, unfortunately, they must live with its consequences. This TalkSheet not only helps validate the feelings of kids who are experiencing or have experienced a divorce, it also gives kids whose parents have not divorced the chance to understand and empathize with their peers who have experienced the tragedy of a marital failure.

To Introduce the Topic:

Write the word *divorce* in large print on a chalkboard or on newsprint for all to see. Walk around the room flipping a coin. Say nothing for a minute or two other than asking kids to call the coin in the air. If they lose the toss, have them sit away from the group. Some in the group may catch on to what you are trying to simulate. After doing this a number of times, explain that this activity is like marriage and divorce. In the United States about half of all marriages end in divorce. (At this writing, there has been a small decline in the divorce rate, and it can be hoped that this trend will continue.) The people sitting away from the group represent those who failed at marriage. If they marry again, their chances of divorcing again are even higher.

You can also successfully introduce this topic using marriage certificates. For this exercise you will need five photocopies of a marriage certificate, one frame, and some tape. Place one of the certificates in the frame, poke one with holes, tear one in several places, tear one into pieces and tape it back together again, and save one to tear later. Hold the certificates up before the group. Explain to the teens that each of these certificates represents a marriage. The framed certificate is the "picture perfect" marriage. The husband and wife care for each other and work hard at keeping the marriage together. The certificate with holes in it signifies a marriage with some problems. There are a few difficulties eating away at it, but so far it has stayed together. The one torn in several places represents a hurting marriage. Perhaps with help it will survive, or this marriage may end in divorce. The certificate torn in pieces but taped together again represents a marriage that has been torn apart but is healing. There are scars, but it can still last. Finally, the last certificate should be held up and torn to pieces. This represents a marriage that has ended in divorce. The certificate of marriage no longer means anything. Pass out the TalkSheets and begin the discussion.

The Discussion:

Item #1: Ask the young people to quickly share their thoughts popcorn style and write each contribution on the chalkboard or on newsprint.

Item #2: This activity gives kids who have never experienced a divorce the chance to better understand what happens. It also lets kids who have experienced the pain share some of it with the rest of the group. Ask several of the group members whose parents have divorced to share their answers.

Item #3: You can role-play these situations so that your group members practice their peer counseling and support skills.

Item #4: Require that young people support their answers with rational reasons. They cannot say "'cause it will be different" or "I'm not like my dad."

Item #5: Let the young people share their different paraphrases. You may want to allow them to work together in groups.

To Close the Session:

Sit in a circle and ask the group members to share one thing they learned from the discussion and one thing they will do differently as a result.

Outside Activity:

Some advance preparation is well worth the effort here. Invite older youths who have lived through a divorce to the meeting to discuss their experiences. Or you might want to interview four to six people about their parents' divorces in advance of this discussion. Tape the interviews and play them for the group.

BETWEEN A ROCK AND A BIBLICAL PLACE

1 Answer each of the following questions.

a. What makes the **most** sense to you about the theory of evolution?

_____

b. What makes the **least** sense to you about the theory of evolution?

_____

c. What makes the **most** sense to you about the theory of creationism?

_____

d. What makes the **least** sense to you about the theory of creationism?

_____

2 What do you think?

	THAT'S RIGHT	THAT'S NOT RIGHT
a. An open-minded person would have to accept evolution as truth.	____	____
b. The Bible and evolution are compatible.	____	____
c. Schools should teach both creationism and evolution as theories in their science courses.	____	____
d. The Bible provides Christians with a scientific account of the origin of the world.	____	____
e. One cannot be a Christian and believe in evolution.	____	____
f. Christians should not study science.	____	____

3 Answer each of the following questions the way you believe the Bible teaches and then the way you believe science teaches.

a. Is there a God?

The Bible says . . . _____

Science says . . . _____

b. How was the world formed?

The Bible says . . . _____

Science says . . . _____

c. How unique are people?

The Bible says . . . _____

Science says . . . _____

d. How do the laws of nature work?

The Bible says . . . _____

Science says . . . _____

4 Each of the following statements summarizes a belief about the origin of life. Choose the one that comes closest to what you believe to be true.

___ **a.** Life evolved through naturalistic processes over a long period of time with no Creator involved.
___ **b.** A Creator created life then allowed that life to evolve through naturalistic processes over a long period of time.
___ **c.** A Creator created life and directed its evolution toward a purpose over a long period of time.
___ **d.** A Creator created life as it exists today and designed all of it for a special purpose.

5 Read each of the following verses that describe God in relationship to the world and everything in it.

Psalm 19:1-6   Colossians 1:16, 17   2 Peter 3:13   Revelation 14:7

How do each of these passages suggest that we interpret scientific data?_____

_____

BETWEEN A ROCK AND A BIBLICAL PLACE
Topic: Science and Creation

Purpose of this Session:

Christian young people progressing through school are confronted with questions and doubts about the validity of their religious upbringing when it appears to conflict with their science classes. This TalkSheet encourages an open and honest discussion on the subject of science and creation. Be sure you set the tone for Christian love, open-mindedness, and safety as young people share their doubts and concerns.

To Introduce the Topic:

Beforehand, tape-record the opinions of different people regarding evolution and creation. Play these for the students and have them react to the views they hear.

You can also introduce the subject by asking the following question: "What would have to happen for algae to evolve into a person?" Let the group members go back and forth in answering this question. They do not need to come to any sort of resolution. Then tell the group you will be discussing the issue of science and creation.

The Discussion:

Item #1: Give volunteers the opportunity to share their answers. Keep the discussion participants from discounting or putting down the views of individuals. So often with hot topics Christian love is thrown out the window in favor of winning an argument.

Item #2: Discuss each statement, allowing time for debate. The following comments can be made to the group after the statements have been discussed. Christianity and science are not competing with each other. They tend to answer different questions. Christianity focuses upon the "why" and "what should be" issues, while science leans toward answering the "how" and "what is" questions. Science examines and tries to explain data. There are more often than not competing theories that explain those data. Creationism is a competing theory with that of evolution. There are a number of creation viewpoints just as there are a number of evolution viewpoints. Many scientific theories of today will be discarded, but God's Word will stand. Scientific theories cannot assert themselves as truth. Since no human being lived to observe the origins of our universe, no scientific models can claim to be truth. By faith, however, we can know that God's Word is truth.

Item #3: The following are brief comments about each statement. **Question a.** The Bible says there is a God who is both infinite and personal. Science says the existence of God can never be proved. **Question b.** The Bible says God created the world fundamentally as it appears now except for the distortions sin has created. Science generally says that the world evolved over millions and millions of years. **Question c.** The Bible says that people have been created in the image of God, making them unique. Science says people are linked to all creation through an evolutionary process that makes all living things similar. **Question d.** The Bible says God created and controls his laws of nature. Science says that nature is controlled by laws that are not influenced by any outside force or power.

Item #4: Allow the young people to share their views. If they come up with an additional view, ask them to write it on a chalkboard or on newsprint for everyone to examine.

Item #5: The passages each describe God as Creator. Explain to the group that all people interpret any information they receive through the filter of their beliefs. If one is an atheist, data will be interpreted differently than if one is a Christian, or if one believes in pantheism. If one believes God created the world, one's view of the world will be affected by that belief.

To Close the Session:

It is beyond the scope of this TalkSheet to discuss the details of the theories of evolution and creation. If you are well versed in these theories, you can debate the merits of each. It is easy to get caught up in subtle details of the theories and models of creationism and evolution, but they have little to do with our faith in Jesus Christ. We make belief in these issues a point of fellowship. Some have made it a question of salvation. The point that needs to be made is that God has declared his involvement in creation—in its beginning, in its sustenance, and in its end. The atheistic interpretations of God's creation or the new age pantheistic interpretations inadequately answer the order, wonder, and complexity of God's creation. Only a view that includes the God of the Bible can adequately explain our world and everything in it. Explain that one has to have as much faith in science to believe its theories as one does to believe in the Bible. Close by reading Psalm 100.

Outside Activities:

1. Have your young people conduct a poll in a shopping mall, asking passersby whether they believe in creation, evolution, or something in between.

2. Ask a scientist who is a Christian or a science teacher to present the different perspectives on the creation/evolution debate.

SEX STUFF

1 What do you think of when you hear each of the following words?

Horny: _____

Lust: _____

The "F" word: _____

Making love: _____

2 Why is a boy considered a stud if he has several sexual partners, but a girl is seen as a slut if she has had the

same number of partners? _____

3 When it comes to sexual attitudes and behaviors, my friends are . . . (*Sexual permissiveness* means how far you go sexually.)

___ more sexually permissive than I am.   ___ less sexually permissive than I am.   ___ about the same as I am.

4 Teenagers base their personal sexual behaviors on what others do.

___ This is **generally true** for people at my school.   ___ This is **not generally true** for people at my school.

5 What do you think? **A = AGREE   NS = NOT SURE   D = DISAGREE**

a. Teenagers abuse sex more than adults.	A	NS	D
b. Teenagers cannot be stopped from having sex.	A	NS	D
c. Sex is as normal as watching TV.	A	NS	D
d. Teenagers should have access to birth control without their parents' permission.	A	NS	D
e. Premarital sex will bring a relationship closer together.	A	NS	D
f. What the Bible says about sex does not matter today.	A	NS	D
g. Sex is okay as long as both people agree.	A	NS	D
h. People who have premarital sex are making a mistake.	A	NS	D
i. There is too much sexual temptation.	A	NS	D

6 Sex education at school has been helpful.

___ This has **been true** for me.   ___ This has **not been true** for me.

7 Complete the following sentence: **A person can decide when it is right to have sex by . . .**

_____

8 Read the Bible verses listed below and describe the sexual attitude and behavior communicated in each.

Job 31:1   Attitude: _____

Behavior: _____

Proverbs 5:18, 19   Attitude: _____

Behavior: _____

Proverbs 6:27-29   Attitude: _____

Behavior: _____

Titus 2:11-14   Attitude: _____

Behavior: _____

Date Used: _____

Group: _____

SEX STUFF
Topic: Sexual Attitudes and Behaviors

Purpose of this Session:
The traditional cultural norm did not used to tolerate premarital and extramarital sexual behavior. Permissiveness was not the norm in our society. The pendulum has swung, however, to the opposite of the traditional cultural norm. No longer is it acceptable to wait until marriage. Young people are encouraged at a young age to express their individuality, including their sexuality. Even in the age of AIDS and herpes, both incurable sexually transmitted diseases at the time of this writing, abstinence is frowned upon and discouraged. This TalkSheet offers young people the chance to dialogue with adults about their sexual attitudes and behaviors and provides you with the opportunity to point out the biblical perspective.

To Introduce the Topic:
Many times males are reluctant to look at a road map when traveling, believing they know where they are going. Only when pressured will they admit they are lost and need directions. The group members can relate to this bit of information if they have traveled with their fathers. Resisting a glance at the road map, these fathers press on toward the land of the lost. Hold up a road map as you are relating this scenario to the young people. Then discuss the attitudes of people who do not want to refer to maps to guide their travel. Tell the group that many people act the same way when it comes to sex. They have created a do-it-yourself manual as their guide instead of referring to God's Word to seek direction. Explain that you wish to talk about some of the attitudes and behaviors that young people have toward sex. Let them know you expect them to behave in a mature fashion and to respect the opinions of everyone involved in the TalkSheet discussion.

The Discussion:
Item #1: Before letting the teens share their responses, go over the ground rules found on page 11. Then talk about the sexual attitudes commonly associated with each of the four words.

Item #2: The double standard persists—permissive sex is acceptable for males, not females. Talk about why the boy should also be considered a "slut."

Item #3: Research indicates that the peer group is a powerful indicator of sexual behavior. If a teenager's reference group is sexually permissive, the teenager will follow that lead. The reverse of this principle is also true.

Item #4: Teenagers like to think they make their own decisions but, generally speaking, their reference groups are the best indicators.

Item #5: These statements will generate a variety of responses. Allow the students to debate the different issues that arise with each. Item "b" is particularly interesting because agreement with this statement is the basis for the widespread promotion of birth control for teenagers.

Item #6: Discuss the pros and cons of school-based sex education.

Item #7: Responses can range anywhere from "when I get married" to "when it feels like it is the right person." Have the group decide upon a sexual standard that most teenagers act upon, and compare it with the biblical standard of abstinence until marriage.

Item #8: Summarize the sexual attitudes and behaviors communicated in each of the passages, and contrast these with the prevailing attitudes and behaviors in society.

To Close the Session:
Review the points explored by the group during the discussion. Challenge the teens to look to God's road map for direction in their sexual lives so that they will not have to wander around lost. Explain that God gave directions in the Bible not because he wanted us to live dull, uneventful lives, but because they teach us the best way to live. Close by reading 1 Thessalonians 4:1-8.

Outside Activity:
Involve your group members in shaping a Christian education series for junior highers on sexuality.

TAKING CARE OF BUSINESS

1 Being responsible = _____

2 Teenagers should not have to be as responsible as adults. (Check only one.)

_____ **True** for all areas of teenage life.   _____ **True** for most areas of teenage life.
_____ **True** for some areas of teenage life.   _____ **Not true at all**.

3 Underline the three top reasons you believe average teenagers give for their irresponsibility.

a. I'm too young.   e. I always have bad luck.   i. I was mad.
b. I forgot.   f. Being responsible is boring.   j. I didn't know any better.
c. There was not enough time.   g. I just don't want to.   k. I couldn't control myself.
d. I'm lazy.   h. It was someone else's fault.   l. I've never learned to be responsible.

4 Place an **X** on each line scale below at the point indicating the degree of responsibility you feel you need to assume for each of the issues. For example, in Item "a" an **X** closest to **No responsibility** would indicate that you do not want to take any responsibility for the quality of your family life. In Item "g" an **X** closest to **A great deal of responsibility** means you do not let your friends dictate whether or not you drink.

a.   **YOUR FAMILY LIFE**
   |____|____|____|____|____|____|____|____|____|
   No responsibility   A great deal of
                                               responsibility

b.   **THE CONDITION OF THE ENVIRONMENT**
   |____|____|____|____|____|____|____|____|____|
   No responsibility   A great deal of
                                               responsibility

c.   **YOUR OWN FEELINGS AND ACTIONS**
   |____|____|____|____|____|____|____|____|____|
   No responsibility   A great deal of
                                               responsibility

d.   **EVANGELISM OF YOUR FRIENDS AND RELATIVES**
   |____|____|____|____|____|____|____|____|____|
   No responsibility   A great deal of
                                               responsibility

e.   **YOUR ALCOHOL/DRUG USE**
   |____|____|____|____|____|____|____|____|____|
   No responsibility   A great deal of
                                               responsibility

f.   **THE PROBLEM OF WORLD HUNGER**
   |____|____|____|____|____|____|____|____|____|
   No responsibility   A great deal of
                                               responsibility

g.   **CHOOSING YOUR GROUP OF FRIENDS**
   |____|____|____|____|____|____|____|____|____|
   No responsibility   A great deal of
                                               responsibility

5 If young people were given more control over their lives, they would be more responsible.

___ **I agree**   ___ **I'm not sure**   ___ **I disagree**

Why? _____

6 Each of the following passages describes a responsibility. Decide how well you are doing with regard to each.

	DOING WELL	SO-SO	NOT SO WELL
Genesis 1:28 Caring for the earth as God's creation.	_____	_____	_____
Exodus 32:22 Not going along with the bad influences of others.	_____	_____	_____
Matthew 25:15 Being a good steward of the abilities God has given to you.	_____	_____	_____
Matthew 27:24 Not blaming others for your responsibilities.	_____	_____	_____
Romans 14:12 Choosing what to do with your life.	_____	_____	_____
Philippians 1:27 Telling others about Christ through your words and actions.	_____	_____	_____

Date Used: _____

Group: _____

TAKING CARE OF BUSINESS
Topic: Teenagers and Responsibility

Purpose of this Session:

Young people report they are acting responsibly. Adults bemoan the irresponsibility of teenagers. Use this TalkSheet opportunity to talk about this all-important growing-up topic.

To Introduce the Topic:

Ask your group members to sit in a circle or circles, if you have a large group. With the room darkened, have one person shine a flashlight (the spotlight) on another's face and fire off questions about responsibility. Only the person in the spotlight may speak. This will focus everyone's attention on the one sharing. The questions can be as deep or as shallow as you wish, and no one is required to answer if he or she is uncomfortable. To begin, ask questions such as, "Do you make your bed?" "How messy is your room?" "How often have you turned in your homework late?" Do not pass judgment on what is said. After several have shared, turn the lights back on and announce you will be discussing responsibility.

The Discussion:

Item #1: Decide upon a group definition of *responsibility*. Possible responses young people will give are doing what you have to do, doing God's will, getting stuff done, meeting your obligations, being accountable for what you do, and doing your duties.

Item #2: Young people want to be treated as if they are responsible *sometimes*. But they do not *always* want adult responsibility. And they want to decide when they get to be responsible and when they get to be irresponsible. Point out the inconsistency of this kind of thinking.

Item #3: Discuss the different reasons why kids shirk responsibility—from blame to distraction.

Item #4: Ask the students to decide what their choices imply. For example, if they choose not to take responsibility for how they feel, do they then have the right to get angry whenever they want? If they do not wish to take some responsibility for the problem of world hunger, are they guilty of murder?

Item #5: Control over our lives is a key contributor to our willingness to take responsibility. It is interesting that young people are asked to take on more responsibility, but they are not given control over the decisions that must be made in relationship to the responsibility.

Item #6: Ask for volunteers to share how they are doing with regard to the responsibilities examined in the Scriptures.

To Close the Session:

Explain to the group that part of our sinful heritage is blaming others rather than taking responsibility. "It's-not-my-fault" thinking began in the garden with Adam and Eve and it remains with us today. No-fault thinking abounds in the adult world. The church board blames the pastor for financial problems, the student blames the teacher for a bad grade, the manager blames the worker for lower productivity, and the parent blames the child for acting up. Point out to the group that shirking responsibility is a worldwide phenomenon. Rich nations do not want to take responsibility for starving ones; warring nations blame each other for their problems.

Responsibility is a matter of perspective. Adults are concerned about teenagers and irresponsibility because they know that in the future acting irresponsibly will not be in the teenagers' best interests. Responsibility is seen by teenagers as part of growing up. They define what they see adults do as maturity. So kids think that drinking and sex make them grown-up. They have confused adult irresponsibility with maturity.

Outside Activity:

Form a panel of parents to answer questions about responsibility from the young people. Ask how young people are ever going to be responsible if they are not given responsibility.

FEEL BADS

1 Place an **X** on the line below indicating where you see yourself.

|_____|_____|_____|_____|

**It does not take much
to get me to feel bad.**

**It takes a lot to
get me to feel bad.**

2 **FEEL BAD SCOREBOARD:** On the line before each of the following, check the ones you have experienced within the last year. Then go back and decide if the event was **A FEEL BAD**, **A BAD FEEL BAD**, or **A REALLY BAD FEEL BAD**.

	A FEEL BAD	A BAD FEEL BAD	A REALLY BAD FEEL BAD
___ Arguing with a parent about rules	___	___	___
___ Feeling far away from God	___	___	___
___ Missing church or church-related activities	___	___	___
___ Breaking up with a boyfriend/girlfriend	___	___	___
___ Arguing with a friend	___	___	___
___ Moving to a different school	___	___	___
___ Being bigger or smaller than most people your age	___	___	___
___ Being bored	___	___	___
___ Conflict with a teacher	___	___	___
___ Parents separating or divorcing	___	___	___
___ Not finishing homework	___	___	___
___ Your parents fighting in front of you	___	___	___
___ Fighting with a parent	___	___	___
___ Getting a bad grade on a test	___	___	___
___ Feeling left out of the youth group	___	___	___
___ Being grounded or restricted	___	___	___
___ Feeling underweight or overweight	___	___	___
___ Feeling frustrated with your Christian life	___	___	___
___ Not having enough time with a parent	___	___	___
___ Being pressured to do something you know is wrong	___	___	___
___ Moving	___	___	___
___ Not being allowed to look or dress the way you wish	___	___	___
___ Arriving late for school or a class	___	___	___
___ Not being good enough for a sport	___	___	___
___ Feeling rejected by a group of people your age	___	___	___
___ Feeling pressured to succeed	___	___	___
___ Getting a bad report card	___	___	___
___ Being nagged by a parent	___	___	___

3 What do you think? **YES, NO,** or **MAYBE SO.**

a. _____ The more teenagers experience the "feel bads" found in Item #2, the less likely they are to trust in Jesus Christ.
b. _____ The more teenagers experience the "feel bads" found in Item #2, the more likely they are to get depressed.
c. _____ The more teenagers experience the "feel bads" found in Item #2, the more likely they are to have problems in the future.

4 How are "feel bads" different for Christians than for non-Christians? _____

_____

5 Read the following Scriptures and write out what you think each verse has to say about "feel bads."

Matthew 11:28-30 _____

2 Corinthians 1:3-6 _____

2 Corinthians 1:8-11 _____

Hebrews 10:23-25 _____

Date Used: _____

Group:_____

FEEL BADS
Topic: Feeling Bad

Purpose of this Session:

Adolescence is about change. Physical, social, mental, spiritual, and emotional changes developmentally affect teenagers. Many life events also create change in the lives of adolescents. These life circumstances can and often do create stress. This TalkSheet was designed to discuss how life events or life stressors often make us feel bad, so it was decided to call them "feel bads." Although many of life's circumstances are positive, they can still create stress, making us feel bad. Take this opportunity to talk about some of life's events, how they make us feel, and what Christians can do about them.

To Introduce the Topic:

This lead-in activity requires either a chalkboard or newsprint. Draw a generic stick figure person large enough for all the kids to see. Explain to your group that you want to look at how feeling bad affects the average teenager. For example, one person may get a stomachache. Draw a line from the stick figure person's stomach (such as it is) out to the side and write *stomachache*. Ask the group to consider all the effects of feeling bad. Some additional examples include a headache, skin breaks out, a dry mouth, grinding teeth, dizziness, lack of hunger, diarrhea, a nervous twitch, heartburn, a backache, cramps, shaky arms or legs, a cold sweat, and an increased heartbeat. Explain to the group you will be talking about life events and how they make us feel. Then pass out the TalkSheets.

The Discussion:

Item #1: Allow volunteers to share stories of life events that made them feel bad. Create a safe environment so that young people feel secure in sharing. Remind the group of your confidentiality rule.

Item #2: Some young people will want to say their life experiences have had no affect on them. Point out that Christians will face life events that make them feel bad. Chapters 1 and 2 of Job describe the "feel bads" that depressed Job. Elijah experienced some positive life events that were "feel bads" for him (1 Kings 19).

Item #3: Discuss each of the statements, debating those that spark controversy.

Item #4: Talk about how common "feel bads" are in everyone's life. Ask how one's hope in Christ can make one's response to them unique.

Item #5: Ask for volunteers to share how they can apply these verses to the "feel bads" they experience.

To Close the Session:

1. Christians will experience "feel bads" just like everyone else.
2. Christians will feel down because of life's circumstances.
3. Discouragement and depression do not have to overcome Christians. Psalm 43 and Psalm 55 speak of the hope we have.
4. Christians can rest assured because we have our hope fixed on the Lord. We may sometimes worry and grow weary over the details of life, but we serve a God who is in control.
5. Be a listener when your friends experience the "feel bads" of life. Both Elijah and Job had friends who supported them when they were down.

Outside Activities:

1. Ask a Christian counselor to attend your group session to talk about life stressors, change, loss, and depression.
2. Ask the group to search the Bible for passages related to hope and comfort.

ECO-CHRISTIANS

 Circle each of the following environmental issues with which you are familiar.

Rain forest destruction	**Air pollution**
Acid rain	**Ozone depletion**
Water pollution	**Species extinction**
Greenhouse effect	**Hazardous waste**
Garbage overload	**Natural resources depletion**

Since the first Earth Day in 1970, environmental problems have lessened.

_____ **True**   _____ **False**

Why?_____

_____

 What do you think? **A = AGREE**   **D = DISAGREE**

a. The earth is our home.	A	D
b. Problems with the environment are a sign of the last days before Christ's return.	A	D
c. Christians and non-Christians alike must repent for their mistreatment of God's creation.	A	D
d. There is a real Mother Earth.	A	D
e. Environmental problems are largely spiritual problems requiring a spiritual change.	A	D
f. Christians have a good record of caring for the earth.	A	D
g. The Bible offers some practical solutions for today's environmental problems.	A	D
h. Teenagers are the best hope available for doing something about environmental abuses.	A	D

 If God were to take you to court, would you be found innocent or guilty of crimes against his creation?

___ Guilty as charged; I deserve a heavy sentence.
___ Guilty, but I'm a first- or second-time offender.
___ Innocent.
___ Innocent by reason of insanity; I did not know any better.

Study the following passages of Scripture and be prepared to discuss them.

Genesis 1:27-30   **Psalm 8**   **Romans 8:18-25**   **1 Corinthians 10:26**

Date Used: _____

Group: _____

ECO-CHRISTIANS
Topic: Christians and the Environment

Purpose of this Session:

Few issues inspire young people to action, but the environment is one issue that has sparked their interest. Western Christianity has a mixed record with regard to the environment. The new age movement's spirituality of monism and pantheism appears to be leading the way in the call for environmental healing. Some new agers have accused Christianity of wreaking havoc on the environment. They cite Genesis 1:27-30 with its theology of dominion as the source of the western world's exploitation of the earth's natural resources. This TalkSheet can be used to give a biblical perspective to environmental issues.

To Introduce the Topic:

Litter the room with pop cans and other safe household trash. When the young people arrive for your group meeting, keep the litter on the floor to use as an illustration during the discussion. Ask the teens how they felt to see so much litter scattered around the room. Did they feel any responsibility to pick up the litter?

The Discussion:

Item #1: Ask for volunteers to define the problem with each of these environmental issues.

Item #2: Generally speaking, the problems have worsened. Not many substantial gains have been made, although people are more aware of the problems.

Item #3: These statements give you an opportunity to talk about a proper Christian perspective on ecology and the environment. Spend extra time on the statement, "Environmental problems are largely spiritual problems requiring a spiritual change." New Agers contend that we must begin to see and appreciate our "oneness" with the earth for healing to occur. God says we must treat what he created with respect because he created it.

Item #4: Hold a brief court hearing and see how your group does.

Item #5: Ask volunteers to share how these passages relate to a Christian perspective on ecology and the environment.

To Close the Session:

The new age movement seeks to bring Eastern thinking to the West. New agers elevate the animal, plant, and mineral world to the level of human beings. They see all things as an undifferentiated oneness, a worldview called *monism*. The wish to elevate this oneness to the level of deity creates the pantheistic view that all is one, all is god. And because all is divine, all should be treated equally. People in India are starving because food is given to cows and rats. In contrast to this, the Bible teaches that people are created in God's image (Genesis 1:26). This gives people value, not because they are god as the new agers contend, but because in fact they are God's creation. People are uniquely divided from the animal, plant, and mineral world. Yet, people are united with that world because all of it was created by God. Because God created everything—the animal, plant, and mineral world as well as humankind—everything has value (Leviticus 25:23; 1 Chronicles 29:14-16; Psalm 50:10, 11; and Haggai 2:8). It is this Christian view that gives creation its meaning. Because God created animals, plants, oceans, and mountains, they are worth respecting. It has been a distorted interpretation of Genesis 1:28 that has given us the idea that the world and all it contains was created for us to exploit. So we have wasted what God intended us to treat with respect. He created us a little lower than the angels and wants us to take care of what he made. We are responsible for creation because of our high position. Sin, however, has separated us from God and has affected creation. The Bible teaches that the whole of creation awaits God's redemption (Romans 8:18-25). While we await God's return to redeem all he made, we are responsible as Christians for what Francis Schaeffer called the "substantial healing" of creation.* We cannot perfect what sin has ruined, but we can go a long way in the healing process.

Outside Activity:

Create a task force using group members, and investigate how your church or parachurch organization can help in the substantial Christian healing that is necessary for God's creation. You may decide upon a paper recycling project or a water conservation plan. There are numerous Christian and secular idea books on the market that outline practical projects designed to help save the environment. They can help your task force generate practical and "doable" ideas.

*Francis Schaeffer, *Pollution and the Death of Man: The Christian View of Ecology* (Wheaton, Ill.:Tyndale House, 1970).

HOLY MASQUERADE

1 Underline up to three words that you believe best describe acts of hypocrisy by the average Christian teenager.

Typical	**Opposite**	**Honest**
Self-righteous	**Sinful**	**Rebellious**
So!	**Two-faced**	**Necessary**
Sad	**Fake**	**Selfish**
Smart	**Intolerable**	**Evil**

2 It is better to believe in Christ and not live the Christian life than to not believe in Christ at all.

_____ **True**   _____ **False**

3 What do you think?   **SA = STRONGLY AGREE   A = AGREE**
                            D = DISAGREE   SD = STRONGLY DISAGREE

a. _____ Adults are more hypocritical than teenagers.
b. _____ Teenagers are forced to be hypocrites by their parents.
c. _____ The church should lower its standards so there would be less hypocrisy.
d. _____ Most people do not see their own hypocrisy.

4 How often do you live what you believe?
___ **Every day**
___ **Most every day**
___ **Some days**
___ **Sundays**
___ **No days**

5 If Christianity is so great, why is it so easy to be a Christian hypocrite?_____

_____

6 How do people who are not Christians act like hypocrites?   _____

_____

7 Read each of the following verses and circle the one that comes closest to describing your life.

Matthew 23:28	**Ephesians 4:22-24**
Romans 7:15-20	**Philippians 2:12, 13**
Galatians 5:19-21	**1 Thessalonians 5:22**

HOLY MASQUERADE
Topic: Personal Hypocrisy

Purpose of this Session:

The charge that the church is full of hypocrites is the classic excuse given for lack of involvement in the body of Christ. During the adolescent years, young people become painfully aware of hypocrisy. This TalkSheet offers the chance to openly and candidly examine the problem.

To Introduce the Topic:

Read examples of hypocrisy from your local newspaper—politicians who are supposed to be civil servants involved in questionable dealings and so on. Ask the kids why these kinds of things occur. This leads into the discussion about personal hypocrisy and Christianity. A hypocrite is one who impersonates or pretends to be someone he or she is not.

The Discussion:

Item #1: Make a master list of the words that your group members underlined. Include additional words they considered while doing the activity. You will quickly identify that personal hypocrisy is a major problem for Christian teenagers.

Item #2: This will most likely prove to be a controversial statement. Ask for volunteers to debate the issue.

Item #3: Pay particular attention to the statement, "Teenagers are forced to be hypocrites by their parents." Ask why many young people believe they are forced by their folks to wear masks. Talk about how young people can assert themselves and still live within their parents' boundaries.

Item #4: This exercise gives young people an opportunity to examine how consistently they practice what they preach.

Item #5: Especially in the United States, it appears to be much easier to be a hypocrite because it is so easy to be religious. This leads to mediocrity and easy shows of belief that are not backed up by lifestyle.

Item #6: Young people need to understand that Christians are not the only hypocrites. Hedonists are hypocrites because they do not totally live out their philosophy. Other religions can claim hypocrites among their ranks as well. Atheists are hypocrites because they often live as if there *is* a creator, yet they claim there is not.

Item #7: The passages describe various degrees of spiritual commitment or lack thereof. Ask for volunteers to share where they see themselves. Your group should provide a degree of safety for some kids to be able to honestly share.

To Close the Session:

One way to look at hypocrisy is to view it as the opposite of repentance. Instead of realizing his or her sin and confessing it, a hypocrite pretends not to need repentance. The hypocrite goes through the Christian motions for the purpose of fooling others or perhaps himself or herself. Young people need to realize that all of us are hypocrites to one degree or another. We are hypocrites every time we judge another (Matthew 7:1). We are hypocrites every time we talk about our sin in the past tense (1 John 1:8). Adults are usually quick to point out the hypocrisy of youths, while youths are quick to point out that adults do not practice what they preach. The Bible warns against being deceived by sin, which gives birth to hypocrisy (Romans 7:11; Jeremiah 17:9; and 1 Corinthians 3:18).

Outside Activity:

Ask several of the students to study hypocrisy throughout the Bible and make a report to the group. They can use a study tool like *Nave's Topical Bible* to help guide their work.

OPPOSITE SEX BLUES

1 When can you first remember wondering about the opposite sex?
(Circle one.)

Before grade school　　　　**Fifth and sixth grades**
First and second grades　　 **Seventh and eighth grades**
Third and fourth grades　　 **High school**

2 If you were to run into a member of the opposite sex at the mall next week, who would you want it to

be? _____　　 Who would you not want it to be? _____

3 Below are a few statements about boys and girls in relationships. Which ones do you feel apply more
to girls? Which ones apply more to boys?

	APPLIES MORE TO GIRLS	APPLIES MORE TO BOYS
Cheating while in a relationship	_____	_____
Pressures to get physical	_____	_____
Preferring to spend time with friends	_____	_____
Possessiveness	_____	_____
Having higher standards	_____	_____
Jealousy	_____	_____
Being domineering	_____	_____
Wanting to get serious quicker	_____	_____
Being committed to God	_____	_____
Leading the other person on	_____	_____
Being romantic	_____	_____
Being demanding	_____	_____
Calling oneself fat or ugly	_____	_____
Being argumentative	_____	_____

4 Can a boy and a girl be close friends without getting serious with each other?

___ **No way**　　　　　　　　　　___ **Probably could happen**
___ **Could happen but not likely**　___ **Sure**

5 **For the boys only:** I can never figure out why girls . . . _____

_____

For the girls only: I can never figure out why boys . . . _____

_____

6 Read the following verses from the book of Ephesians and decide what they have to say to teenagers
about relating to the opposite sex.

Ephesians 4:2 _____

Ephesians 4:25 _____

Ephesians 4:29 _____

Ephesians 4:32 _____

Ephesians 5:1 _____

Ephesians 6:18 _____

Date Used: _____

Group: _____

OPPOSITE SEX BLUES
Topic: Relating to the Opposite Sex

Purpose of this Session:
The battle of the sexes rages on, but need this be the case for Christians? Maybe so, but you can help bridge the understanding gap with this TalkSheet designed to help Christian young men and women better relate to each other. As teenagers progress through the adolescent years, they learn to develop mature opposite sex relationships. Dialogue between the sexes can help young people with this important, God-given developmental stage. (See also "SEX STUFF," page 71.)

To Introduce the Topic:
Play "Spin the Bottle" with a slight twist. Instead of laying a kiss on a random player, the spinner gets to ask whomever the bottle points to at the end of its spin a question about the opposite sex. You can use an empty plastic 32-ounce soda bottle for the spinner.

The Discussion:
Item #1: This should prime the memories of your group and generate a variety of stories. Give the adults involved in your youth group discussion the opportunity to share their memories as well.

Item #2: Young people may describe both their romance stories as well as tales of horror. Point out that both are part of relating to the opposite sex. Brainstorm reasons why people have these romantic and horror stories. Begin exploring ways young people can relate as friends without all the unhealthy entanglements that often occur.

Item #3: Wow! The discussion sparks will fly when you look at these. Examine the differences and similarities between the sexes. Decide how many are cultural and how many are God-given. In order to push kids to think, the choice "Applies equally to girls and boys" was not given. But you will want to give this option as you discuss the exercise.

Item #4: This has always been a topic of discussion between young men and women. Romance is the issue that divides friendships between the sexes, although many teenagers believe they do have close friendships without serious involvement. The problem arises when one person in the relationship begins to fall for the other, but the feelings are not mutual. Discuss what kinds of friendships Christian young men and women can have and how these can be developed.

Item #5: Use this opportunity to answer questions that arise from completing these sentences. It can be fun for the boys to answer the girls' questions and vice versa.

Item #6: Have volunteers share what they learned. Then ask the group to describe a boy-girl relationship that might exist if these Scriptures were lived out.

To Close the Session:
Because young women and men have so many questions and concerns about the opposite sex, you will have undoubtedly covered much ground in your discussion. Emphasize that there are both differences and similarities between the sexes, and as Christians we can celebrate them both. Focus on the "one another" passages found in Ephesians, and challenge your young people to have friendship relationships with the opposite sex that are not romantically based. These friendships flourish best in groups, which is one of the many reasons youth groups exist. You can wrap up the discussion by brainstorming ways your group can encourage nonromantic relationships that focus on serving Christ and others.

Outside Activity:
There are a number of Christian books that have been published about the differences between the sexes. Obtain several different ones from your local Christian bookstore and have group members investigate what the authors say about the differences and the similarities. Have them report their findings to the group.

WALKIN' WITH GOD

1 How often do you think about each of the following?

	A LOT	SOME	A LITTLE	NEVER
a. Wanting a closer relationship with God.	___	___	___	___
b. Wishing you could actually see God.	___	___	___	___
c. Wondering how closely God is listening to your prayers.	___	___	___	___
d. Feeling that something is missing in your relationship with God.	___	___	___	___
e. Considering questions about God and Christianity that do not seem to have any real answers.	___	___	___	___
f. Wondering if all this Christian stuff is a waste of time.	___	___	___	___
g. Wishing you could understand God.	___	___	___	___

2 What do you think? **YES**, **NO**, or **MAYBE SO.**

_____ If you know about God, you know God.
_____ You should feel closest to God at church.
_____ Getting to know God is quite difficult.
_____ Pastors feel closer to God than others.
_____ There is no one correct way to grow in a relationship with God.
_____ If Christ had not become a human being, we could not have a personal relationship with God.

3 Suppose you were one of the 12 disciples of Christ. Do you think that as one of the disciples, you could have known God more personally than you do now? ___ **Yes** ___ **No**

Why or why not? _____

_____

_____

4 How is your relationship with God like a friendship? _____

_____

How is your relationship with God unlike a friendship?_____

_____

5 From the following passages, write one thing each teaches about personally relating with God.

Psalm 84:2 _____

Psalm 89:46 _____

Isaiah 6:3-7 _____

John 1:18 _____

Colossians 1:21-23 _____

Hebrews 2:14 _____

Hebrews 4:14-16 _____

Date Used: _____

Group:_____

WALKIN' WITH GOD
Topic: Knowing God More Personally

Purpose of this Session:

Young people want to know God—not know about God, but *know* God. They want a personal relationship with him. They want to see him, talk with him, and walk with him. Take this opportunity to discuss personal, intimate relationships with God.

To Introduce the Topic:

Shoes can be an interesting lead-in to your discussion. For this activity you will need to collect shoes from several age groups. You can bring in a pair of baby booties, toddler prewalkers, preschool running shoes, elementary school dress shoes, high school basketball high tops, and adult dress shoes. Beginning with the baby shoes, hold up each pair of shoes. Tell the group that these shoes are a reminder of growth. As we grow up, we grow out of our shoes. The dress shoes that looked nice on a second grader would not even fit a freshman. Then tell your group that our relationships with God also change as we grow. As children, God is an extension of our parents, an older father-type figure or maybe a Santa Claus. Now that they are teenagers, they have a more complex understanding of God. They now understand that they can have a more personal relationship with him.

The Discussion:

Item #1: Let volunteers share their doubts, interests, and longings for a relationship with God. Point out that the psalmist felt the same way (Psalm 42).

Item #2: Debate each of these statements. Point out to the group that knowing God is not as easy nor is it as hard as we make it out to be. God is as close to us as our next prayer.

Item #3: We like to think that if we lived in New Testament times our faith in Christ would be different. But the New Testament good old days were not so good, just old. Read Matthew 28:17.

Item #4: You will not find the phrase "personal relationship with Jesus Christ" in the Bible. Yet, God does reveal to us through other terminology that he desires our friendship. Let the group members share their insights into how a relationship with God is like and unlike a friendship.

Item #5: Ask volunteers to share what they learned from each passage. Create a master list to record the insights of the group.

To Close the Session:

Point out to the group that the metaphor of walking with God is a useful way to look at how we relate to him. There are different ways we walk with people. For example, if you go to the mall with your parents, you might walk away from them. You don't want your friends to see you so close to them. When walking with a boyfriend or a girlfriend, you might hold hands or walk arm in arm. If you have the unfortunate experience of walking with a police officer to be questioned for a crime, you might walk with your head lowered. While with your friends you might walk casually and coolly as you talk. Ask the kids to describe how they are walking with God. Then read the following bumper sticker to them: If you don't feel close to God, guess who moved.

Outside Activities:

1. Encourage your group members to keep spiritual journals of their relationships with God. For one week they are to write down their thoughts and feelings about God. Good times for journaling would be as they pray, read the Bible, worship, or reflect in the evening on the day with God. They may want to write a poem, compose a prayer, draw a picture, or write a narrative. At your next meeting kids can share their thoughts and feelings about their journaling experiences. Some of them may find they enjoy journaling and will continue to do so.

2. An excellent book about a personal relationship with God is Tim Stafford's *Knowing the Face of God* (Zondervan, 1989).

FIBS, LITTLE WHITE LIES, AND OTHER HALF-TRUTHS

1 People seem to divide lies into two kinds: little white lies and real lies. Give two examples of each that the average person would classify as little white lies and real lies.

LITTLE WHITE LIES	REAL LIES
a. _____	a. _____
b. _____	b. _____

2 There are times when one has no choice but to lie to a parent.

___ **This is true.**   ___ **This is a lie.**

Why?_____

_____

3 Decide which, if any, of the following would justify telling a lie.

a. ___ To get you out of trouble   f. ___ To stay in lying practice
b. ___ To protect a friend   g. ___ To cover for your parents
c. ___ To boost your self-image   h. ___ To hide a painful past experience
d. ___ To avoid hurting another's feelings   i. ___ To keep a secret
e. ___ To get something for yourself   j. ___ To save someone's life

4 React to the following statement: **There is a difference between lying and not telling all of the truth.**

___ I strongly agree.   ___ I am not sure.   ___ I strongly disagree.
___ I agree.   ___ I disagree.

5 Think about the last time you lied.

a. Was it easier to tell the lie or to tell the truth? _____

b. What could you have done to avoid the lie? _____

c. What happened because you lied?_____

d. How comfortable did you feel telling the lie?_____

e. Do you believe your own lies?_____

6 What is one lie you wish you could untell? _____

_____

7 Choose one of the following Scriptures to rewrite in your own words:

Psalm 5:6 _____

Proverbs 19:9 _____

Ephesians 4:25 _____

Colossians 3:9 _____

Date Used: _____

Group:_____

FIBS, LITTLE WHITE LIES, AND OTHER HALF-TRUTHS
Topic: Lying

Purpose of this Session:

Some teenagers tell the truth, some lie to escape painful consequences. Some say they must lie, some lie when it would be easier to tell the truth. Lying is a common strategy young people use to navigate their way through adolescence. God was clear in Scripture about the dangers of lying, yet young people often have difficulty seeing the consequences of their deception. Use this TalkSheet to explore this often confusing issue.

To Introduce the Topic:

A good lead-in is to play the game "Whopper." Have the young people write three statements about themselves, two of which are true and one that is not. The rest of the group members try to guess which of the three is a lie. If the young people choose two truths that sound like lies and a lie that sounds plausible, they will be successful in fooling the group.

Another introductory strategy is to ask the group the following question: "If you were to be hooked up to a lie detector, would you agree to answer any question your parents asked you? How about any question your youth pastor asked you? Your best friend? Your boyfriend/girlfriend?" Then process why they would or would not submit to the lie detector test.

The Discussion:

Item #1: Ask the group to clarify the difference between a little white lie and a real lie. Many people honestly believe that their lies are harmless, especially those little white lies that people feel are necessary for survival. The rationale in telling these lies is that the intention behind it is good. Therefore the lie cannot be that bad. The important but often unasked question is how do we know that our good intentions will in fact turn out good?

Item #2: Lying to parents and other authority figures to escape disciplinary action is often seen as acceptable. Teenagers think in the immediate, not in the past or the future. The here and now is where they live. So lying as a survival strategy appears effective in the present. But God is clear that he hates lying. The Lord gave us guidelines for living that work for the long haul. The following are biblical examples of lying out of fear (Genesis 18:15), lying in order to avoid trouble (Matthew 28:13, 14), and lying to look religious (Acts 5:1, 2).

Item #3: Each of the reasons listed are perceived payoffs for lying. It is easy to confuse a payoff with a justification for lying.

Item #4: Ask the group if omitting some of the truth is the same as lying.

Item #5: Have different group members volunteer to answer the questions. When kids say they cannot remember the last time they lied, discuss why we tend to block out the sins we have committed.

Item #6: There is no need to ask the young people to share their lies aloud. Instead, ask them to reflect on what they learned from reviewing a lie they wish they could untell. What damage was done by the lie?

Item #7: Ask some of the young people to read aloud their personalized versions of the Scriptures. Choose one or two to discuss in depth.

To Close the Session:

Lying gives us a false sense of control and power. We may feel we have managed a situation successfully, but our perception is illusionary. Lying is like microwave popcorn. The little kernels sit peacefully in their package, but when the microwave heats them up, the package grows bigger and bigger. When the heat of daily living is on, we sometimes lie. But like the package of popcorn, the lies grow and grow until finally they become unmanageable.

Outside Activity:

Construct a simple three- to four-question poll. Have your group conduct the poll in a shopping mall, asking the passersby whether they think lying is right or wrong. Bring the results back to the group and examine them together.

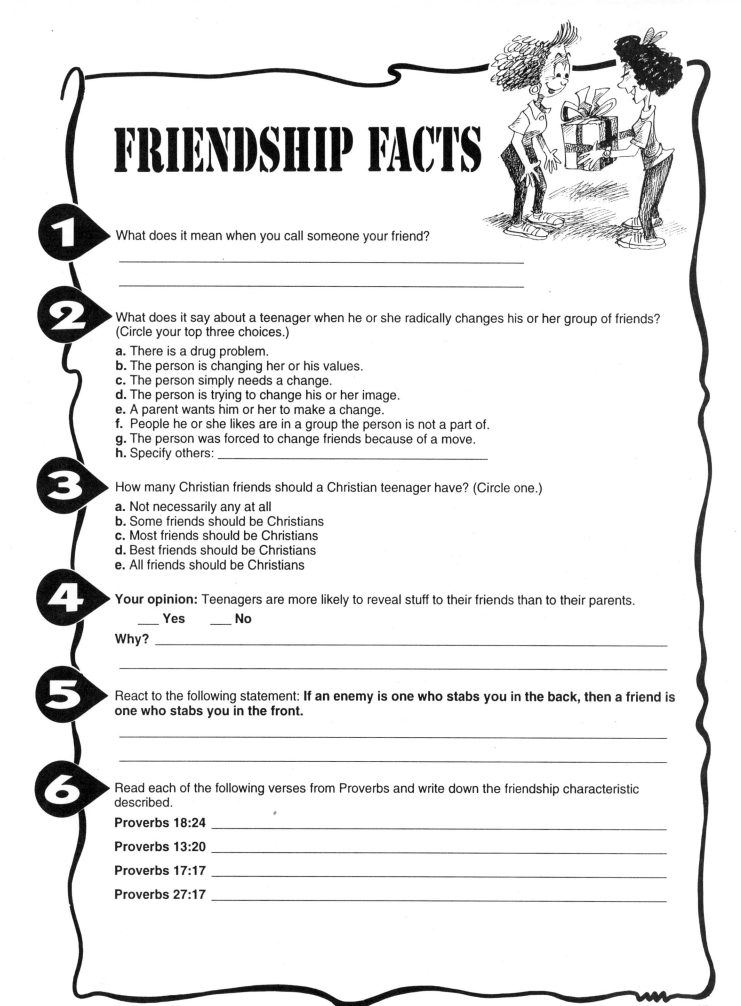

FRIENDSHIP FACTS

1 What does it mean when you call someone your friend?

_____

_____

2 What does it say about a teenager when he or she radically changes his or her group of friends? (Circle your top three choices.)

a. There is a drug problem.
b. The person is changing her or his values.
c. The person simply needs a change.
d. The person is trying to change his or her image.
e. A parent wants him or her to make a change.
f. People he or she likes are in a group the person is not a part of.
g. The person was forced to change friends because of a move.
h. Specify others: _____

3 How many Christian friends should a Christian teenager have? (Circle one.)

a. Not necessarily any at all
b. Some friends should be Christians
c. Most friends should be Christians
d. Best friends should be Christians
e. All friends should be Christians

4 **Your opinion:** Teenagers are more likely to reveal stuff to their friends than to their parents.

___ **Yes**   ___ **No**

Why? _____

_____

5 React to the following statement: **If an enemy is one who stabs you in the back, then a friend is one who stabs you in the front.**

_____

_____

6 Read each of the following verses from Proverbs and write down the friendship characteristic described.

Proverbs 18:24 _____

Proverbs 13:20 _____

Proverbs 17:17 _____

Proverbs 27:17 _____

Date Used: _____

Group: _____

FRIENDSHIP FACTS
Topic: Friends

Purpose of this Session:

Friends are the lifeblood of adolescence. What teenager has not had friend troubles? Kids learn valuable lifelong lessons from friendships, grow in Christ through friends, get into trouble because of friends, and fall in love with friends. Obviously friends are important, so it is vital that you and your teens discuss their questions and concerns.

To Introduce the Topic:

Tell the young people they will be creating a "recipe of friendship." Hand out a copy of a conventional recipe (like chocolate chip cookies) or write it on a chalkboard or a large sheet of paper. Break into small groups and explain that they are to use this format to invent a recipe for friendship. It might be helpful to brainstorm and write down all the words the group can think of that apply to friendship. Words such as *love, caring, honesty, trustworthy, confrontation, sharing,* and so on may be suggested for the groups to choose from as they write their recipes. Encourage uniqueness and creativity. When the recipes are completed, have the group members exchange recipes and read them to the group.

The Discussion:

Item #1: Make a list of everyone's contributions. Survey the list and ask the group how much commonality there is among the group's responses.

Item #2: Young people change friends frequently for a variety of reasons. Some reasons are good, while others are bad. Discuss how kids can know when they are making changes for the worse.

Item #3: Answers will vary greatly on this one. Stay away from lecturing kids about the importance of Christian influence. Rather, share your own positive experiences regarding support and direction from Christian friends.

Item #4: Some parents are more understanding and "askable" than others. Encourage your kids to have friends and still maintain dialogue with their parents.

Item #5: Discuss the importance of honest feedback from friends. This is one way you can tell you have a friend—your enemies will stab you in the back, while your friends will be up front and let you know how they honestly feel.

Item #6: Ask volunteers to read the passages and share the friendship characteristic taught.

To Close the Session:

Close by reviewing some of the "one another" passages found in Scripture.

Love one another	**Don't hold grudges toward one another**	**Carry one another's burdens**
John 13:34, 35	Matthew 5:22	Romans 15:1
John 15:12, 13		Galatians 6:2
Romans 12:10	**Forgive one another**	James 5:16
Ephesians 5:1	Ephesians 4:31, 32	
Hebrews 13:1	Matthew 18:21, 22	**Serve one another**
1 Peter 4:8		Galatians 5:13
	Pray for one another	Ephesians 5:21
	Ephesians 6:18, 19	1 Peter 4:9, 10
Discipline one another	James 5:16	
Galatians 6:1		**Worship with one another**
Matthew 18:15		Psalm 95:6
2 Thessalonians 3:14, 15	**Be patient with one another**	
Hebrews 12:15	Ephesians 4:2	

Outside Activity:

Obtain the names and addresses of another church's youth group members. This group may be either across town or across the country. Have each member of your group choose a name of the same gender and write a letter of introduction to his or her new pen pal.

AN X-RATED WORLD

1 How did you react when you first saw the parental advisory warning shown on the left?

2 In one sentence write your definition of *obscene*.

Obscene **means . . .** _____

3 List one reason why each of the following is so popular with young people.

a. Rock music with sexually explicit lyrics: _____

_____

b. Comedians who use filthy material: _____

_____

c. The use of profanity in movies: _____

_____

4 What do you think?   **A = AGREE   D = DISAGREE**

a. Popular entertainment (movies, TV, rock music,comedy) contributes to the moral
decline of our culture.   **A   D**
b. There is very little anyone can do to restore a higher standard of decency to our society. **A   D**
c. Raw language is so common today that it is meaningless.   **A   D**
d. There should be no censorship whatsoever.   **A   D**
e. Rock music is becoming more X-rated.   **A   D**
f. Obscenity laws should be strictly enforced.   **A   D**
g. Christians should be more active in condemning the obscene in the culture in which they live. **A   D**
h. Those reacting negatively to pop entertainment are simply showing their prudishness. **A   D**

5 How would you respond if you were in each of the following situations?

a. Riding home from school with four friends, the driver of the car plays a cassette with a sexually violent theme.

_____

b. A friend gives you a vulgar "safe sex" T-shirt for your birthday. _____

_____

c. While at a novelty gift shop at the mall, a friend shows you a greeting card with a naked body on it. _____

_____

d. A bedroom scene is shown on a soap opera you are watching with friends after school._____

_____

6 Read the following Scripture verses and write down what you think each verse has to say about living in an X-rated world.

1 John 2:15-17 _____

Philippians 4:8, 9 _____

James 4:4 _____

AN X-RATED WORLD
Topic: The Obscene and Pop Culture

Purpose of this Session:

Our pop culture bombards people with the crude, the profane, the lewd, and the filthy on a daily basis. Because young people are particularly affected by the pop culture of the day, this X-rated assault is numbing them to the obscene. What was particularly offensive only a generation ago hardly raises an eyebrow today. Unfortunately, the commonality of the obscene is being protected under the guise of freedom of expression. This TalkSheet affords you the opportunity to dialogue with young people about the profound affect the obscene in the pop culture is having on them.

To Introduce the Topic:

To illustrate how common the obscene has become in your community, make a list with your group of the obscene things in the pop culture. The list could include excerpts from cable TV, rock music concerts, pornographic shops, or examples from your local schools.

The Discussion:

Item #1: Many young people as well as adults see the parental warning and quickly scan the TalkSheet to find the sexually explicit material. Some are offended just seeing the warning label. Take a minute to discuss why people are attracted to such a label. Point out that the more available objectionable material is, the more likely people will be to read it, watch it, and listen to it.

Item #2: Discuss the different definitions people have of *obscene*. Many kids will mention sex in their definition. Make sure you point out that sex and obscene are not the same. Read a dictionary definition of the word. *Webster's New World Dictionary* defines it as "offensive to modesty or decency; lewd."

Item #3: Let a number of group members share their opinions. Ask the group how involved teenagers are in the world of pop culture/pop entertainment (movies, music, comedy, under-21 teen night clubs, rock concerts, and the like).

Item #4: Open these statements up to debate, especially if a difference of opinion exists. Several of the questions will promote discussion around the idea of how much society should tolerate. Expect the First Amendment question of freedom to be raised. The First Amendment is quoted below in case you want to refer to it. Ask the group if the First Amendment guarantees total freedom or if society has the right to restrain certain things.

> Congress shall make no law respecting an establishment of religion, or prohibiting the free exercise thereof; or abridging the freedom of speech, or of the press; or the right of the people peaceably to assemble, and to petition the Government for a redress of grievances.

Item #5: These mini tension getters make great role-play situations as well as discussion starters on how to handle everyday situations involving the obscene. Ask the teens to share their own tension getters that they have faced. The group can brainstorm Christian responses to these difficult but real dilemmas.

Item #6: Philippians 4:8, 9 is a wonderful passage that can serve as a litmus test to help Christians evaluate the culture. Discuss with the group members how this verse applies to the pop culture that surrounds them. If time allows, move to the other two passages for discussion.

To Close the Session:

Point out that standards of decency have eroded because society has allowed them to erode. The obscene no longer exists on the fringes of culture but has become the mainstream. But is that what Christians want? Is that what society wants? Our X-rated, four-letter culture will continue its decline as long as it is allowed. Challenge the students to take a positive stand in their personal lives when it comes to the obscene and pop culture. You can use an example from the computer world. GIGO (garbage in, garbage out) is a phrase used to explain what happens when a computer programmer programs a computer incorrectly—only worthless information comes out. The same applies to society and individuals. What good can possibly come from putting the obscene into one's life?

Outside Activity:

The Supreme Court uses the following three measurements to determine if something is obscene:*

OBSCENITY TEST

1. The dominant theme of the material taken as a whole appeals to a prurient interest in sex.

2. The material is patently offensive because it affronts contemporary community standards relating to the description or representation of sexual matters.

3. The material is utterly without redeeming social value.

Write the obscenity test on newsprint large enough for the group to see. Tell the teens that according to Supreme Court rulings, for material to be considered obscene and thus not protected by the First Amendment, it must pass all three of the tests independently. Use this obscenity test to decide what might need to change in your community. You may want to use some of the examples generated from your introduction. Some additional examples are movie rental stores, rock concerts, 1-900 phone numbers, card/novelty shops, cable TV, and schools. Discuss with the students how much of the obscene they think Christians should tolerate in your community.

*This obscenity test is quoted from 383 United States Report, *Memoirs* v. *Massachusetts*, p. 413.

WOULD YA, SHOULD YA, COULD YA?

1 Answer the following question: **What might be different if the Ten Commandments had been called the Ten Suggestions?**

_____

2 On the lines before each of the following situations, write the letter **A** (Always), **S** (Sometimes), or **N** (No way).

a. _____ If you went to a party and realized marijuana was being smoked, you would leave immediately.
b. _____ If you were collecting money for the food bank in your area with two other friends and they tried to talk you into keeping some of the money to go play video games, you would do it.
c. _____ If you were given the chance to cheat on a history test, you would take the opportunity.
d. _____ If you were asked to contribute money to help a friend get an abortion, you would donate something.
e. _____ If your parents grounded you from the mall, you would go there behind their backs.
f. _____ If you had clothes you no longer wanted, you would donate them to the Salvation Army or another charity.
g. _____ If you had to do a book report, you would write something based on watching the movie.
h. _____ If you were asked to volunteer time to work at a homeless shelter, you would look into doing it.

3 What do you think? **A = AGREE   NS = NOT SURE   D = DISAGREE**

a. A decline in moral values is the number one problem facing the country.	**A**	**NS**	**D**
b. Females are more moral than males.	**A**	**NS**	**D**
c. There is a great difference between what young people truly believe about right and wrong and what young people think they are supposed to believe.	**A**	**NS**	**D**
d. Young people are more concerned about not getting caught doing wrong than trying to do the right thing.	**A**	**NS**	**D**
e. When deciding right from wrong, people must decide for themselves.	**A**	**NS**	**D**
f. Young people understand the difference between what is right and what is wrong.	**A**	**NS**	**D**

4 If you were to talk with a seventh grade Sunday school class about morality, what would you tell them about how to know the difference between right and wrong? _____

_____

5 Read each of the passages and complete the sentences.

Ecclesiastes 7:20 No one can do right all the time because _____

_____

Mark 10:31 Christ turns the world's values around by _____

_____

Luke 3:7, 8; 11-14 Right living means _____

_____

Ephesians 2:1-5 Being dead in our sins means we should now _____

_____

1 John 2:15-17 Christians need to reject the world's values because _____

_____

Date Used: _____

Group:_____

WOULD YA, SHOULD YA, COULD YA?
Topic: Morality

Purpose of this Session:

The conceptions of what moral means to today's adolescents are varied and blurred. What is right and what is wrong has become distorted and convoluted. Parents and the church must become more intentional in teaching values and moral standards. This TalkSheet offers you just that opportunity.

To Introduce the Topic:

Have the members play tug-of-war. A rope is not necessary if the boys sit in a circle with their arms and legs locked together while the girls try to pull them apart. Follow up the game with the comment, "Trying to decide right from wrong is a lot like tug-of-war. You can feel pulled in two directions." After the introduction, pass out the TalkSheets.

The Discussion:

Item #1: Talk about why God gave us commandments. Ask the question, "Were they meant to make our lives miserable or were they given because this is the best way to live our lives?" Explore why more and more people are living contrary to God's way and the present and future consequences of doing so.

Item #2: Each of these brief tension getters can help your group explore morality in practical situations. You can also refer back to these when you wrap up the discussion.

Item #3: Poll the students on each of the statements. If everyone agreed on a particular one, go on to the next. If there is a wide difference of opinion, have a pro and con discussion.

Item #4: See if the kids can back up what they say with biblical support.

Item #5: Each of the passages address Christian morality. Ask several volunteers to complete the sentences, then discuss what they had to say about Christian morality.

To Close the Session:

Summarize what has been said during the TalkSheet discussion. Tell the group members that their beliefs and behaviors today will have a profound effect on their present and future lives. Morality or the lack of it still matters even though it is in decline. God gave us commands not to ruin our lives but because these guidelines are the best way to live. Challenge the teens to choose God's way as their way. Choosing his way is choosing life (Deuteronomy 30:15-18).

Outside Activity:

Ask the kids to record how many of the Ten Commandments are broken in the next TV program they watch. The next time the group gets together, individuals can share their findings and discuss the implications of societal disregard for God's morality.

GOD THOUGHTS

1 How do non-Christian teenagers you know view God? (Circle the two most popular.)

a. They don't believe there is a God.
b. They believe there are many gods.
c. He's a big policeman in the sky.
d. He's a nice old man.
e. He's the guilt guy.
f. He's a wimp.
g. He's a permissive parent.
h. Other: _____

2 God seems like this to me.

	MOST OF THE TIME	SOMETIMES	HARDLY EVER OR NEVER		MOST OF THE TIME	SOMETIMES	HARDLY EVER OR NEVER
a. Personal	____	____	____	**v.** Kingly	____	____	____
b. Healing	____	____	____	**w.** Blameless	____	____	____
c. Eternal	____	____	____	**x.** Accepting	____	____	____
d. Strong	____	____	____	**y.** Merciful	____	____	____
e. Angry	____	____	____	**z.** Passive	____	____	____
f. Remote	____	____	____	**aa.** Cruel	____	____	____
g. Just	____	____	____	**bb.** Restrictive	____	____	____
h. Loving	____	____	____	**cc.** Worthless	____	____	____
i. Caring	____	____	____	**dd.** Protective	____	____	____
j. Unchanging	____	____	____	**ee.** Good	____	____	____
k. Liberating	____	____	____	**ff.** Forgiving	____	____	____
l. Mysterious	____	____	____	**gg.** Feeble	____	____	____
m. Holy	____	____	____	**hh.** Honest	____	____	____
n. Controlling	____	____	____	**ii.** Pure	____	____	____
o. Punishing	____	____	____	**jj.** Patient	____	____	____
p. Unapproachable	____	____	____	**kk.** Influential	____	____	____
q. Sinless	____	____	____	**ll.** Kind	____	____	____
r. Giving	____	____	____	**mm.** Unaware	____	____	____
s. True	____	____	____	**nn.** Demanding	____	____	____
t. Friendly	____	____	____	**oo.** Critical	____	____	____
u. Involved	____	____	____	**pp.** Sovereign	____	____	____

3 Choose three of the words from Item #2 that you feel seem to describe God most of the time for you. Fill in the three blanks below with your three words and then complete each of the sentences.

a. If God is _____, then this means . . . _____

_____

b. If God is _____, then this means . . . _____

_____

c. If God is _____, then this means . . . _____

_____

4 The prophet Isaiah provides a rich description of God. Read the two short descriptions, one that describes God and one that describes false gods, and write out what you learned:　　**Isaiah 44:6-8**　　**Isaiah 44:9-20**

_____

_____

_____

Date Used: _____

Group: _____

GOD THOUGHTS
Topic: Views of God

Purpose of this Session:

The Bible says that "no one has ever seen God" (John 1:18), yet the Bible is filled with metaphorical descriptions of him. In 1913, Freud postulated that people's God concepts were projections of their images of their fathers. Research on this subject has tended to discount this assertion, but it persists. This TalkSheet helps your kids explore their conceptions of God through discussion.

To Introduce the Topic:

Ask for two volunteers to help you introduce this topic. One person should stand away from the group facing the chalkboard or a large piece of newsprint. This person is the artist. The other person, the interpreter, should stand facing the group with his or her back to the artist. Give the interpreter an object like a light bulb or a coat hanger. The interpreter then explains the object to the artist in such a way that he or she can accurately draw a picture of it. The interpreter cannot look at the artist nor can the artist look at the interpreter. Talk about how such a drawing is like our conception of God.

The Discussion:

Item #1: Take a poll to find out the most popular view of God from a non-Christian teenager's perspective. How difficult does this make it to have friendships with them? How has your group tried to give them a different view of God?

Item #2: This is not a scientifically validated test, but your students can get an idea of how they view God by comparing their responses to the following list. Write the list on the chalkboard or on newsprint. Have the group members write down the headings on the backs of their TalkSheets. Under each heading have them write down the descriptive words that they checked under the category "most of the time." The heading that has the greatest number of descriptive words is the predominant view they have of God. Again, this is not scientifically accurate, but it will generate some interesting discussion.

CONDEMNING	RELATIONAL	RIGHTEOUS	REDEMPTIVE	POWERFUL	DISTANT
Angry	Personal	Holy	Forgiving	Strong	Remote
Controlling	Friendly	Good	Healing	Eternal	Feeble
Punishing	Kind	Just	Liberating	True	Mysterious
Critical	Loving	Pure	Accepting	Unchanging	Worthless
Demanding	Involved	Honest	Giving	Sovereign	Unapproachable
Cruel	Protective	Sinless	Merciful	Influential	Passive
Restrictive	Caring	Blameless	Patient	Kingly	Unaware

Item #3: The way we view God affects how we view life. If we see God as unapproachable, then we will not take prayer seriously. If we see God as critical, then we will be hard on ourselves. Let volunteers read their completed sentences, then discuss how our God thoughts affect our actions.

Item #4: Ask the teens to share the different things they learned from the prophet Isaiah about the one, true God and false gods.

To Close the Session:

Challenge the group members to rethink their views of God. Most of us have a narrow perception of God, which limits what God can do in our lives. God commanded us not to worship idols (Exodus 20:3-6) because he knew that our distorted views of him would limit what he could do with us and what we could do with him. Suggest to the students that they write a large G in the margin of their Bibles every time they find something about God. Then every time they open their Bibles they will begin to see descriptions of God that they can review.

HOTLINE TO HEAVEN

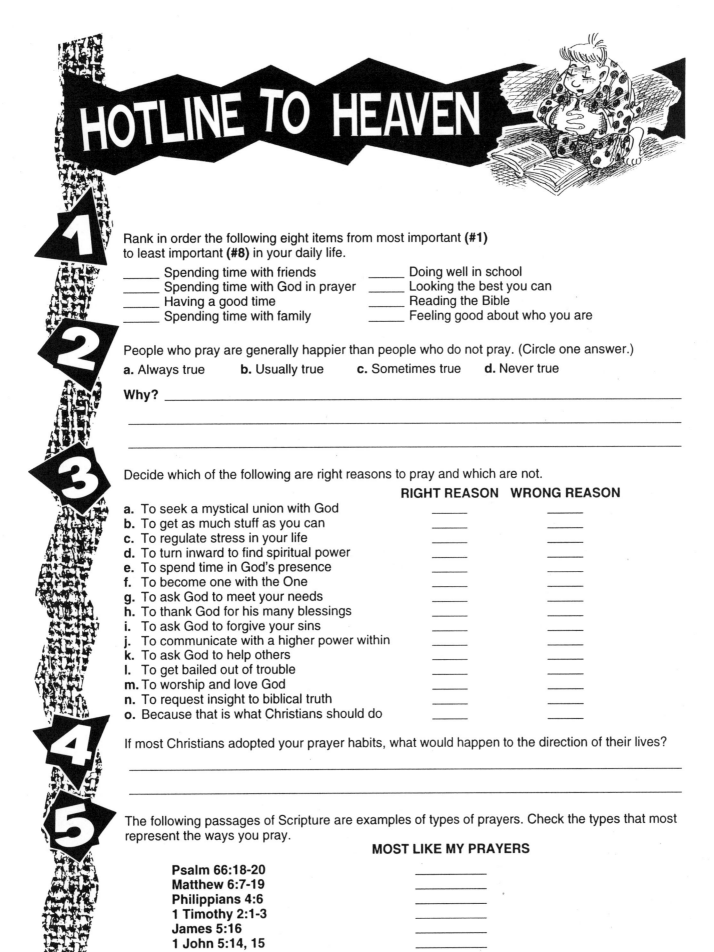

1 Rank in order the following eight items from most important **(#1)** to least important **(#8)** in your daily life.

_____ Spending time with friends   _____ Doing well in school
_____ Spending time with God in prayer   _____ Looking the best you can
_____ Having a good time   _____ Reading the Bible
_____ Spending time with family   _____ Feeling good about who you are

2 People who pray are generally happier than people who do not pray. (Circle one answer.)

a. Always true   **b.** Usually true   **c.** Sometimes true   **d.** Never true

Why? _____

_____

_____

3 Decide which of the following are right reasons to pray and which are not.

	RIGHT REASON	WRONG REASON
a. To seek a mystical union with God	_____	_____
b. To get as much stuff as you can	_____	_____
c. To regulate stress in your life	_____	_____
d. To turn inward to find spiritual power	_____	_____
e. To spend time in God's presence	_____	_____
f. To become one with the One	_____	_____
g. To ask God to meet your needs	_____	_____
h. To thank God for his many blessings	_____	_____
i. To ask God to forgive your sins	_____	_____
j. To communicate with a higher power within	_____	_____
k. To ask God to help others	_____	_____
l. To get bailed out of trouble	_____	_____
m. To worship and love God	_____	_____
n. To request insight to biblical truth	_____	_____
o. Because that is what Christians should do	_____	_____

If most Christians adopted your prayer habits, what would happen to the direction of their lives?

_____

_____

5 The following passages of Scripture are examples of types of prayers. Check the types that most represent the ways you pray.

MOST LIKE MY PRAYERS

Psalm 66:18-20	_____
Matthew 6:7-19	_____
Philippians 4:6	_____
1 Timothy 2:1-3	_____
James 5:16	_____
1 John 5:14, 15	_____

Date Used: _____

Group: _____

HOTLINE TO HEAVEN
Topic: Prayer

Purpose of this Session:

Prayer—we talk a lot about it, but we don't do much of it except when we are in trouble. Prayer is a basic Christian discipline. Young people need to know the importance of talking and listening to God. Examine the critical need for prayer in the life of the Christian by having a TalkSheet discussion on the subject.

To Introduce the Topic:

Bring in a doorknob sign from a hotel or motel room. Usually on one side it says "do not disturb," while the flip side states "maid service." Ask the group how this doorknob sign is like prayer. Usually we have the "do not disturb" side facing outward to God. When we make a mess of things, we flip the sign over to "maid service" and ask for help in picking up the pieces.

The Discussion:

Item #1: Ask the kids to compare their rankings with the reality of their lives. How far up on the importance ladder should prayer be? If their perception of the importance of prayer versus the reality of prayer in their daily lives is inconsistent, explore the reasons why.

Item #2: Does prayer have much to do with happiness and the quality of one's life? Many Christians who take prayer seriously say yes! Check out what your kids think.

Item #3: The following statements are examples of new age thinking. They need to be identified and discussed because they can deceive kids into wrong thinking about prayer.

1. To seek a mystical union with God.
2. To regulate stress.
3. To turn inward to find spiritual power.
4. To become one with the One.
5. To communicate with a higher power within.

Item #4: Have kids share their personal prayer experiences. Use this item to evaluate the quality of the group's prayer life as well as the quantity.

Item #5: Discuss the different types of prayer examples found in the passages of Scripture.

To Close the Session:

Get into a circle or circles depending upon the size of your group. Tell the kids you want to have popcorn prayers. Each member of the group prays a one word or one phrase prayer to God. This type of praying is like popping popcorn because you quickly move around the group just like popcorn is rapidly bounced around its container. Decide in advance how many times around the circle you will go. Examples would be *thanks, caring, parents, loving youth group*, and so on.

Outside Activity:

Your youth group activities calendar can double as a prayer calendar. The next time you create your calendar, print the names of kids and adults involved in your group in each of the daily squares. Somewhere on the calendar provide instructions so that kids understand that on different days they are to pray for the specific person whose name appears. Hand out the calendars and encourage your students throughout the month to keep up their prayer support for members of the youth group.

READY, SET, GROW

1 How would your life be different if you were not a Christian?

_____

_____

_____

2 Circle each of the following things that have helped you grow as a Christian.

Sharing the Gospel message with others	**Feeling guilty often**
Serving others in Christ's name	**Praying**
Tithing money to the church	**Confirmation**
Trying hard not to sin	**Attending church**
Walking your talk	**Saying spiritual things**
Sharing in fellowship with Christian friends	**Reading the Bible**
Worshiping God	**Reading Christian books**
Church membership	**Memorizing Bible verses**
Deep Bible study	**Baptism**
Confessing sins	**Attending youth group**
Asking questions	**Discussing with other Christians**

3 What do you think?

	THAT'S ME	THAT'S NOT ME
a. I have spent time trying to understand my Christian faith.	_____	_____
b. I pray in other places besides church.	_____	_____
c. I have talked with another Christian about my questions regarding Christianity.	_____	_____
d. When I have a problem, I consider how Jesus might want me to handle it.	_____	_____
e. I read my Bible in places other than church.	_____	_____
f. I have talked with my friends about what it means to be a Christian.	_____	_____
g. I am regularly involved in my church's activities.	_____	_____
h. I have helped someone in need during the past month.	_____	_____
i. When I have a life decision to make, I talk it over with God.	_____	_____
j. Christianity is one of the most important influences in my life.	_____	_____
k. I have experienced God's love and forgiveness.	_____	_____
l. I realize I need God's continual grace and love.	_____	_____
m. I attend church more than once a week.	_____	_____

4 The person I know who is most like Jesus Christ is _____. I think I can

become more like Jesus by _____.

5 Study one of the following passages of Scripture and be prepared to discuss it.

1 Corinthians 13:12	**1 Corinthians 14:20**	**2 Corinthians 3:18**
Hebrews 5:11-14	**Ephesians 3:17-19**	**Ephesians 4:14, 15**

Date Used: _____

Group: _____

READY, SET, GROW
Topic: Christian Growth

Purpose of this Session:

Wow! What a big topic for discussion. Christian growth is becoming like Jesus. Since none of us has done it yet, and none of us is an expert, this discussion can powerfully motivate and contribute to Christian growth. Everyone in your group can be a resource to help everyone else grow in Christ.

To Introduce the Topic:

This introductory activity requires you to collect books for a variety of age groups. You will need baby books (with only pictures and one or two words per page), preschool books, elementary school readers, a high school novel, and a college textbook. Hold up the books and ask your group who might be reading each type of book. Explain to your group that Christian growth is like the books you have displayed. Just as kids progress up the reading levels, we can progress in becoming more like Christ. Pass out the TalkSheets and begin your discussion.

The Discussion:

Item #1: Let the kids hypothesize what their lives might be like without Christ. Some kids will think it would be improved, others will see no difference. Allow all the kids to share without being put down. Kids rebelling against Christ or apathetic kids need support. This activity lets you know where your kids are in their relationships with Christ. You can then facilitate the discussion more productively knowing where your group stands.

Item #2: Do not set up right or wrong answers. Let the teens share and debate what has been helpful as well as what has hindered their becoming more like Jesus.

Item #3: Ask kids to resist telling the group what they think the group wants to hear. Encourage honesty and role-model support as the students examine their own lives.

Item #4: A Christian growth role model can be helpful to young and old alike. If we see that others are growing more like Christ, we realize that we can, too. Ask volunteers to share why their chosen people are most like Christ. Create a master list of all the ways in which the group can become more like Christ.

Item #5: Ask which passage they would like to discuss first. Focus your attention on that choice. Continue to study each passage as time permits.

To Close the Session:

When we talk about Christian growth, we typically focus upon the individual's responsibility to become more like Jesus. But we grow in Christ through community as well as individually. That is one reason for the establishment of the church. The context of our growth is the living body of Christ, with Christ the head. Take time to close the session by examining with the young people how the church can better promote their Christian growth.

Outside Activity:

Challenge your teens to chart their individual spiritual growth over the past year. You will need to pass out a piece of graph paper and a marker to each group member. Have each person draw a straight line across the center of the page. This line will represent the last year of the teen's spiritual life. It should be labeled like the example below.

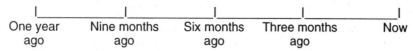

| I_____I_____I_____I_____I |
| One year | Nine months | Six months | Three months | Now |
| ago | ago | ago | ago | |

    The line itself is a baseline. The area above the line represents spiritual growth. The area below the line represents a spiritual slump or stagnation. Beginning with one year ago, have the kids draw lines representing their spiritual progress. Significant points, high or low, should be indicated by a cross and a comment. For example, a week at camp may be marked with a cross and a comment about its significance. Hanging around with a negative friend may drop the line below the baseline. When they are done, have the kids share their spiritual progress with the group.

IS YOUR CHRISTIANITY COLOR-BLIND?

1 Place an **X** somewhere on the Racism Scale below that best describes your opinion.

- **There is more racism today than in the past year.**
- **There is about the same racism today as in the past year.**
- **There is less racism today than in the past year.**

2 **YES** or **NO?**

___ Have you ever talked with a member of another race about race relations?
___ Would you be willing to talk to a member of another race about Jesus Christ?
___ Do you know someone of another race fairly well?
___ Would you feel comfortable working together on a school or church project with a member of another race?
___ Would you want to be close friends with a member of another race?

3 What do you think?

	AGREE	NOT SURE	DISAGREE
a. Teenagers are less racist than adults.	___	___	___
b. Minorities are as racist as whites.	___	___	___
c. Whites are in debt to blacks and other minorities because of past discrimination and injustice toward them.	___	___	___
d. Whites are afraid of minorities.	___	___	___
e. There is more racism directed toward blacks than other minorities.	___	___	___
f. Churches have little to offer minorities.	___	___	___
g. Minorities should quit blaming their problems on whites and do something to help themselves.	___	___	___
h. A doctrine of equality cannot be found in the Bible.	___	___	___
i. Minorities must work harder to get along with whites than whites must work to get along with minorities.	___	___	___

4 It has been said that the Sunday church service is the most segregated hour in America. How true is this for

your church? _____

_____

5 Is the God of Christianity too white? _____

_____

6 Read the following Scripture verses and write out what you think each passage has to say about racism.

Matthew 28:19 _____

Luke 12:7 _____

Galatians 3:28 _____

James 2:8, 9 _____

Revelation 4:11 _____

Date Used: _____

Group: _____

IS YOUR CHRISTIANITY COLOR-BLIND?
Topic: Racism

Purpose of this Session:
You say race relations are not so good? Then use this TalkSheet to take a look at the state of race relations in your community and your church. Many of us, young and old alike, verbalize our lack of prejudice and discrimination but commit acts of bigotry. Racism persists as a problem around the world. But Christians can reject racism and call others to treat everyone with the dignity and respect they deserve as creations of God.

To Introduce the Topic:
Bring different colored markers of different sizes and shapes to the group. Point out that these markers represent the different races. Have the teens discuss how these markers are like different people. You will find the group pointing out things like different heights, weights, shapes, and colors, but make note that all were created to mark. You may even get some racist remarks mixed into the group observations. Write all the observations down using the markers. Then point out that the group will be talking today about how we view certain races differently, just like we noted the differences in the marking pens. This same introduction can also be done effectively with different kinds of sodas or fruit juices. Pour the different kinds of juices into various sized clear containers. Then ask the kids to make their observations.

The Discussion:
Item #1: Reproduce the scale on the chalkboard or on newsprint. Take a poll of the young people's opinions and group their responses on the scale to get a picture of your group's perception of racism. Ask the students to volunteer different examples of racism evident at their schools. Examples might be racially motivated fights, jokes, name-calling, discrimination, or racial harassment.

Item #2: Many youths have not had much personal contact with other races. The more personal and positive contact one has, the less racism persists. Ask the students to share why (or why not) they may feel uncomfortable in close relationships with other races.

Item #3: Discuss the statements the teens do not all agree on. If there is one that causes a lot of argument, let them debate the issue. Divide them into dissenting groups, and give them time to formulate a case for their positions before they begin. Encourage them to use biblical support for their opinions.

Item #4: During the time of slavery, Christians supported slavery through a distorted view of Christianity and misuse of the Bible. They taught that the curse on Ham (Genesis 9:18-27) was a curse by God on blacks. How is Christianity and the Bible misused today to maintain a racist attitude and behavior among white Christians? Why should the whites in churches take the initiative to end racism?

Item #5: Malcolm X once said, "Christianity is the white man's religion." Explore why blacks and other minorities might perceive this to be true. Ask what Christians can do to demonstrate God's grace toward all people. Point out that Billy Graham once said that he believed in Christ, not in Christianity.

Item #6: Let the group members share their interpretations, then focus on one passage to study. Relate to the group the story of the Good Samaritan (Luke 10:25-37) in which Christ condemns the Jews' hypocrisy as well as their bigotry. The Samaritans were hated by the Jews, yet Jesus points to the Samaritan as the one who demonstrated love and mercy.

To Close the Session:
God is opposed to racism in whatever form it takes. Scripture makes this clear, but unfortunately the American church has a mixed record in standing against the sin of racism. This does not, however, discount what God says about it. In the Old Testament God taught the people of Israel that the alien and the Jew were equal in God's eyes. All people were created by God and should be treated equally (Numbers 15:15). Christians should oppose racism and discrimination and live in such a way that people of all races will be drawn to God's redemptive, nonracist love.

Outside Activity:
Ask the group to conduct a Sunday school class or a group discussion that focuses on examining what the church's role should be in erasing racism.

BIBLE DOCTRINESZZZZZ

1 | Bible doctrine = _____

2 | It doesn't matter what you believe as long as you are a Christian.
___ **I agree**   ___ **I disagree**

3 | Circle each of the following that you believe are Bible doctrines.

Agnosticism	**Baptism**	**Inspiration**	**Pantheism**	**Reconciliation**
Amillennialism	**Creationism**	**Islam**	**Perseverance**	**Redemption**
Anarchy	**Deism**	**Justification**	**Pessimism**	**Sanctification**
Angelology	**Hedonism**	**Mysticism**	**Petrification**	**The Second Advent**
Atonement	**Incarnation**	**Nihilism**	**Propitiation**	**The Trinity**

4 | Go back to Item #3 and put a triangle around the three words you want to know more about.

5 | Answer the following question: **How can Bible doctrines make a difference in your life?**

_____

_____

6 | Read each of the following passages of Scripture and write down what you believe they have in common.

       John 7:16, 17   **Romans 6:17**   **2 John 9, 10**

       Ephesians 4:14   **1 Timothy 1:3-6**

_____

_____

_____

_____

_____

_____

_____

_____

_____

BIBLE DOCTRINESZZZZZ
Topic: The Study of Bible Doctrines

Purpose of this Session:

There is a great deal of time spent on high-interest topics, such as those found in this book. But relatively little time is spent on the major doctrines developed throughout the Bible and identified by the church fathers as important. This TalkSheet examines Bible doctrines and helps your kids identify some they wish to study.

To Introduce the Topic:

Bring a bottle of insect repellant to the group, and ask why you might need to apply it. Explain that the Bible is like insect repellant because it can protect us from the false beliefs and teachings that lead us astray. Many Bible teachings have been organized into themes or groups of teachings about God and his kingdom.

The Discussion:

Item #1: Bible doctrines are Bible themes or teachings about God and his kingdom.

Item #2: Engage the group in a debate regarding the importance of what one believes and how that affects one's Christian life.

Item #3: The following are all Bible doctrines: amillennialism, angelology, atonement, baptism, creationism, incarnation, inspiration, justification, perseverance, propitiation, reconciliation, redemption, sanctification, the Second Advent, and the Trinity.

Item #4: Some kids will joke around with this one. Once everyone is serious, take a closer look at Bible doctrines by using a Bible dictionary. Look up the terms that are not Bible doctrines.

Item #5: Examine how beliefs affect the way we live. For example, if you believe in reincarnation, your outlook on life will be different than if you believe in a heaven and a hell.

Item #6: Boil down the theme of the passages into a one-sentence statement about the importance of sound Bible doctrine.

To Close the Session:

Refer back to the introductory activity and point out that obviously you cannot apply insect repellant just once. It must be applied each new day you venture out. So, too, must we apply the Bible and its themes or doctrines. Continuous study will protect us from the crazy and wild beliefs rampant in today's society.

Outside Activity:

Ask group volunteers to each take one of the Bible doctrines found in Item #3 and study it using Bible tools, such as a Bible dictionary. They could look up the Scriptures and follow the doctrine throughout the Bible. Give a specified time for the volunteers to report back to the group.

THE D WORD

1 From the list below, circle those you know who have died. Place a **C** on the line before each of the those with whom you were close.

___ Friend   ___ Pet

___ Teacher   ___ Neighbor

___ Parent   ___ Sunday school teacher

___ Grandparent   ___ Student at school

___ Brother/sister   ___ Coach

___ Other relative   ___ Other: _____

2 Teenagers often share common feelings about the death of someone they knew. Underline what you believe are the five most common responses to the death of a loved one.

Shock	**Denial**	**Hurt**	**Confusion**
Fear	**Numbness**	**Relief**	**Depression**
Anger	**Acceptance**	**Guilt**	**Sadness**
Regret	**Helplessness**	**Loneliness**	**Emptiness**

3 Do you **AGREE** or **DISAGREE**?

	AGREE	NOT SURE	DISAGREE
a. Death is something teenagers need not worry much about.	___	___	___
b. Teenagers distance themselves from old people because old people are closer to death.	___	___	___
c. Most people are not prepared to die.	___	___	___
d. People who have a purpose in life have less fear of death.	___	___	___
e. Teenagers have difficulty talking about death.	___	___	___

4 Death is a natural part of the life cycle.

___ **True**   ___ **False**

5 Read the following Scriptures to find out God's perspective on death.

     Psalm 16:10   **1 Corinthians 15:54-57**

     Psalm 49:10-19   **2 Corinthians 5:6-10**

     Isaiah 57:1, 2   **Hebrews 2:14, 15**

Date Used: _____

Group: _____

THE D WORD
Topic: Death

Purpose of this Session:

Young people are increasingly preoccupied with death—in their music, through the suicide of a classmate, or in the contemplation of the meaning and purpose of life. But death is difficult to discuss in a death-denying culture like the United States. This TalkSheet faces death in a straightforward manner. By talking about death, you are provided with the opportunity to talk about eternal salvation.

To Introduce the Topic:

Place the following list of words on a chalkboard or on newsprint for the whole group to see: *mortuary, graveyard, funeral, hospice, mourning, wake, undertaker, embalm,* and *cremation.* Each of these words should be placed around the word *death.* Ask for the young people's reactions to these words.

The Discussion:

Item #1: Let kids share some of their emotions about their experiences. Many kids who have been touched closely by death have not been afforded the opportunity to grieve over their loss. Be sensitive to young people in mourning!

Item #2: Continue the opportunity of sharing. Emotional responses from the previous activity can spill over into this one. Be particularly sensitive to the issue of suicide.

Item #3: These statements should generate some good healthy debate. Have the kids share their opinions on each one, and give reasons why they feel the way they do.

Item #4: The New Testament (Romans 5:12-14; 1 Corinthians 15:26) teaches that death is our enemy though we need not fear it. It is not a part of the natural life cycle. Death proves the reality of sin and evil. Most young people will answer true to this item. Allow a healthy debate to occur. Ask that those debating this issue find scriptural support for their positions.

Item #5: Using these and other passages of Scripture, have the group put together a theology of death.

To Close the Session:

Review the ground the group has covered. Use this closing time to emphasize that the life of each individual involved in this TalkSheet discussion has meaning. It is God who gives our lives meaning. Because of Christ's work on the Cross, each of us can be saved from the despair of a meaningless life and ultimate death. Death stares all of us in the face. We may try to turn our backs on it through the pursuit of pleasure or hard work, but death cannot be denied forever. Through the salvation offered by the Lord Jesus Christ, we can pass from death to life—a life everlasting (John 5:24).

The media sensationalize death as violent, unbelievable, or dramatic to the point that young people are desensitized regarding death. It is almost viewed as an unreal occurrence, only happening to an unfortunate few. But death is very real. The new age movement has anesthetized people to the reality of death with a focus on reincarnation and testimonials of near-death experiences. They report moving toward the light, coaxed on by a mysterious guide, and of seeing loved ones who have died. This denial of the finality and tragedy of death brought on by sin only serves to confuse young people. Only through a relationship with Jesus Christ can death be viewed realistically.

Outside Activity:

Ask a funeral director to talk with your group about her or his experiences with families who have had a loved one die. The teens can also ask questions they have about everything from embalming to burial.

SMUT WORLD

1 Justice Potter Stewart of the U.S. Supreme Court said that he could not define pornography but, "I know it when I see it." What would be your definition of *pornography*?

_____

_____

_____

2 What do you think? **A = AGREE**   **NS = NOT SURE**   **D = DISAGREE**

a. Young people who view pornography will be unaffected.	A	NS	D
b. Limiting the publication, distribution, and sale of sexually explicit material amounts to censorship.	A	NS	D
c. Television programming contains visual material that could be considered pornographic.	A	NS	D
d. A person can become addicted to pornography.	A	NS	D
e. The increase in sex crimes like rape and incest can be partly blamed on the widespread availability of sexually explicit material.	A	NS	D
f. Only child pornography should be outlawed.	A	NS	D
g. Most pornography is harmless.	A	NS	D
h. Pornography encourages violence toward females.	A	NS	D
i. The viewing of sexually explicit material should be legal for people over the age of 21.	A	NS	D
j. The more a person is exposed to sexually explicit material, the less likely that person is to develop a healthy sexual outlook.	A	NS	D

3 I would not rent movie videos at a store that also rented sexually explicit videos.

___ **That's true for me.**
___ **It depends.**
___ **That's not true for me.**

Why? _____

_____

_____

4 Why do you believe pornography has been renamed *adult entertainment*?

_____

_____

5 Study one of the following passages of Scripture and be prepared to discuss how it relates to the issue of pornography.

1 Corinthians 6:9-11	**1 Corinthians 10:11-13**
1 Corinthians 10:31-33	**Ephesians 4:20-24**
James 1:13-15	**1 John 2:15-17**

Date Used: _____

Group: _____

SMUT WORLD
Topic: Pornography

Purpose of this Session:

Pornography is widespread and available to most teenagers who really want it. The tragedy of adolescent involvement is seen daily in the offices of Christian counselors. Their adult clients tell stories of addiction to pornography, of becoming sexually aware as children because of pornography, and of other tragedies directly and indirectly related to their introduction to pornography as children and adolescents. Use this TalkSheet to explore this painful and tragic topic.

To Introduce the Topic:

Write the following ways young people are introduced to pornography on a chalkboard or on newsprint:

Computer "porno" graphics	Telephone 900 numbers	R-rated movies
National Geographic	Soft-core pornography magazines	*Sports Illustrated* swimsuit edition
Playboy or *Playgirl*	Pornographic videos	Hard-core pornography magazines
X-rated movies		

Ask the young people to identify the top three ways youths are introduced to pornography. They can add to the list you have created. Tell the group that just as there are gateway drugs (caffeine, nicotine, and alcohol) that introduce young people to mind-altering drugs and the drug world, there is gateway pornography that introduces young people to the world of smut. Tell the group that this TalkSheet focuses upon the issue of pornography. Review the ground rules found in the introduction of this book. Many more young people than we often realize have been adversely affected by pornography.

The Discussion:

Item #1: You may want to have a dictionary available to look up the word. Ask the group why Justice Potter Stewart's words ring true—because pornography is something you see that arouses sexual desire. A sixteenth-century painting of a nude does not appeal to the prurient desires, but a pornographic magazine does. Ask the group the following question: "How helpful is it to look at pornography?"

Item #2: Discuss each of these statements, letting the teens express their thoughts on each one. Allow time for disagreements. Once you have completed the discussion, poll the students to determine if they feel that pornography is generally harmful, has mixed effects, or is generally harmless. You can further explore this by asking what harm might come to the average teenager who has only casual exposure to pornography.

Item #3: This is a tough issue that most people who rent video movies have never explored.

Item #4: Talk about how the makers of pornography have been able to get mass acceptance by making it sound fun, mature, and harmless. Is this a good label to give pornography?

Item #5: Ask the kids which passage they would most like to discuss first. Focus your attention on that choice, asking the group to relate it to the issue of pornography. As time permits, address each of the other five passages.

To Close the Session:

Summarize what has been discussed during the session, pointing out that pornography desensitizes its consumers to a healthy view of sex. Pornography distorts the Christian view of love, commitment, and fidelity. It promotes promiscuity and an exploitive view of both men and women. Emphasize the compulsive side of the pornography problem. Involvement begins slowly but for some people it progresses into an addiction.

Outside Activity:

Ask a Christian counselor familiar with the addiction process and pornography to speak with your group. He or she can answer questions the young people have and also discuss some case studies. Instruct your speaker not to include graphic examples in the case studies. Your intention is not to be pornographic in discussing pornography but to talk about the pain and sorrow associated with the victims of pornography.

GETTING GOOD AT CHURCH

1 Chart your involvement in church on the graph to the right.

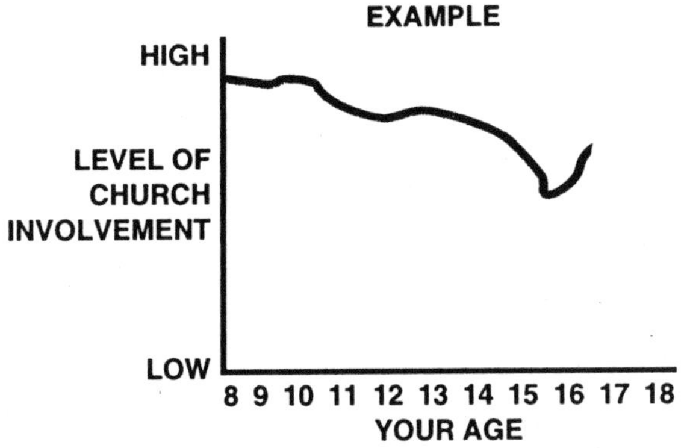

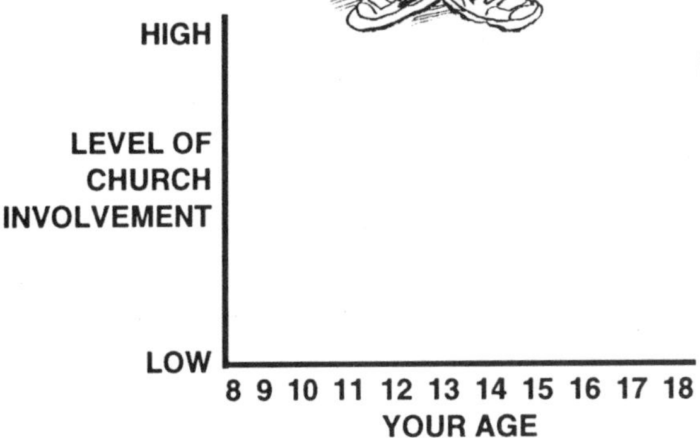

EXAMPLE

HIGH

LEVEL OF
CHURCH
INVOLVEMENT

LOW

8 9 10 11 12 13 14 15 16 17 18
YOUR AGE

HIGH

LEVEL OF
CHURCH
INVOLVEMENT

LOW

8 9 10 11 12 13 14 15 16 17 18
YOUR AGE

2 Predict your future **adult** involvement in church by placing a check on the line before each of the following statements that you think will apply to you.

___ I will regularly attend church services.
___ The church will be an important part of my life.
___ I will be involved in a number of church activities.
___ I will take a leadership role in church.
___ I believe my involvement in church will be a great source of life satisfaction.
___ I plan to marry someone who sees church involvement as important.
___ I will encourage my future family's involvement in church.
___ I plan to be in a full-time ministry position as a career choice.

3 How have your parents affected your involvement in church?

Mother: _____

Father: _____

4 Your opinion, please!   **A = AGREE   D = DISAGREE**

_____ **a.** Attending church most of your childhood makes living the Christian life easier as a teenager.
_____ **b.** It is normal for teenagers to rebel against the church.
_____ **c.** It is the church's responsibility to motivate a teenager's involvement in church.
_____ **d.** A teenager should be allowed to attend a different church than that of his or her parents.
_____ **e.** Parents and their teenage children need to agree on spiritual matters.

5 Place an **X** on the scale below, indicating where you presently see yourself.

|_____|_____|_____|_____|_____|_____|_____|

Committed to   **Rebelling against**
church   **church**

6 Revelation 2:1-3:22 describes the condition of seven churches. Examine your own life and relationship with God by choosing which condition comes closest to describing your personal spiritual condition.

_____ **a.** Church in Ephesus: Read **Revelation 2:1-7**   _____ **e.** Church in Sardis: Read **Revelation 3:1-6**
_____ **b.** Church in Smyrna: Read **Revelation 2:8-11**   _____ **f.** Church in Philadelphia: Read **Revelation 3:7-13**
_____ **c.** Church in Pergamum: Read **Revelation 2:12-17**   _____ **g.** Church in Laodicea: Read **Revelation 3:14-22**
_____ **d.** Church in Thyatira: Read **Revelation 2:18-29**

Date Used: _____

Group: _____

GETTING GOOD AT CHURCH
Topic: Church Involvement

Purpose of this Session:

Church—some young people love it, others do everything they can to get out of it. If your kids are like most, they are at different stages of church commitment. Use this activity to talk about church involvement in a nonthreatening manner. Let kids who are openly rebelling against attending church speak their minds. Let young people who are excited and actively involved share their stories and encourage the discouraged and angry. Maintain an open environment where the Holy Spirit can work in the lives of all the teens, no matter what their commitment level.

To Introduce the Topic:

Divide your students into small groups and have a contest to see which group can come up with the best excuses for missing church. Give the groups three minutes to work. Ask them to share some of the most interesting ones.

The Discussion:

Item #1: Replicate the graph on a chalkboard or on newsprint. Ask different group members to come forward, chart their church involvement, and share what the chart says about their spiritual lives. Have the group give them feedback and encouragement.

Item #2: Provide the kids an opportunity to share their predictions about their own church involvement in one, five, and ten years.

Item #3: Some young people are made to attend church, while others attend in spite of their parents. Examine how the group as a whole has been affected by their parents' church involvement. Ask if they will follow their parents' example if they choose to have children.

Item #4: Vote on each of these statements, debating any controversial issues that come out of the discussion. The statement "Attending church most of your childhood makes living the Christian life easier as a teenager" warrants additional discussion. Too many young people compartmentalize their Christianity. They have not been challenged nor have they seen Christianity lived out in all areas of life. Many young people feel that going to church as a kid prepares one for going to church as an adult, period.

Item #5: Create an atmosphere in which kids can truthfully share their answers and get support rather than alienation.

Item #6: You can also use this activity as a group to examine your church or churches. For every problem that is brought up, ask the group to also suggest a solution as well as how they can be a part of that solution.

To Close the Session:

The word *church* in the New Testament is *ekklesia* from the words *ek*, out of, and *klesis*, called. The word then describes Christians as ones who are called out. The church is an assembly of Christians who have been called out of the world as witnesses for Jesus Christ. We are a community of believers even though we do not always act as one. Point out that the Bible uses several word pictures for the church—*a body, a building, a family*, and *a bride* (a body—Romans 12:4, 5; a building—Ephesians 2:21, 22; a family—Romans 8:17; and a bride—2 Corinthians 11:2, 3). Ask the teens to tell how your church is like each of these. Then ask if your young people feel a part of these. Are they part of the body? Do they feel the love of the family of God?

Encourage the group members to continue their involvement in building up the body, the building, the family, and the marriage.

Outside Activity:

Windshield flyers have long been used as a way to advertise an event, a product, or a program. You can also use the production of a flyer as a discussion activity. You will need sheets of construction paper, markers, and some sample business flyers. Explain to your students that they are in charge of publicity for a church. They must first create a church situation. They can be as imaginative as they wish, as long as it reflects a church that could realistically exist. Then they should design a windshield flyer that advertises the church of their creation. Have each group share its flyer and talk a little bit about its dream church.

HOMOPHOBES

1 Do you know someone who is a homosexual (male or female)?
___Yes   ___ Maybe   ___ No

2 *Homophobia* is a word used to describe the fear of homosexuals demonstrated by many heterosexuals. See if you can name three fears young people have of homosexuals.

Fear #1: _____

Fear #2: _____

Fear #3: _____

3 How do you feel about homosexual activity between consenting adults who love each other?
___ God approves of it, and so do I.   ___ God disapproves of it, and so do I.
___ God approves of it, but I do not.   ___ God disapproves of it, but I do not.

4 What do you think?   **A = AGREE   D = DISAGREE**

a. Homosexuality is a choice.	**A**	**D**
b. A practicing homosexual could not be a Christian.	**A**	**D**
c. Homosexuality cannot be changed.	**A**	**D**
d. The church must reach out to evangelize and disciple more members of the homosexual community.	**A**	**D**
e. Homosexuals are not much different than you or I.	**A**	**D**
f. Heterosexual sex outside of marriage is just as much a sin as homosexual sex.	**A**	**D**
g. Homosexuals should be willingly accepted into the church.	**A**	**D**

5 If you discovered that a friend or an acquaintance of yours was a homosexual, what would you do?
___ Tell my friend that he or she is doing the right thing.
___ Never talk to my friend again.
___ Stay friends.
___ Try to talk him or her out of it.
___ Be as supportive as possible but explain that I think it's wrong.
___ Suggest my friend seek counseling from a homosexual counselor.
___ Tell him or her to get tested for AIDS.
___ Other: _____

6 What would happen in your church if a Christian homosexual were to openly and publicly share his or

her need for Christian love and forgiveness? _____

_____

7 Read each of the following Bible verses. Circle those that apply to the sin of homosexuality. Underline those that apply to the homosexual person.

Leviticus 18:22	**Leviticus 20:13**	**Luke 19:9**
Romans 1:27, 28	**Romans 5:8**	**Romans 8:35**
Romans 15:13	**1 Corinthians 6:9, 10**	**Ephesians 3:18, 19**

Date Used: _____

Group: _____

HOMOPHOBES
Topic: Homosexuality

Purpose of this Session:

God has called the church to be a redemptive community. Yet the church is also the defender of moral values. And in a postmodern world with collapsing values, homosexuality presents a thorny dilemma. How can the church be redemptive to the homosexual and still uphold its defense of strong moral values? The tendency of most churches is to defend a high moral standard rather than to create a loving redemptive community. So the church becomes the homosexual's judge rather than a helper. Adults in the church, for the most part, have accepted the church's stand without much debate. But today's young people are growing up in a generation more tolerant of alternative lifestyles. The gay liberation movement began at a homosexual bar in New York in 1969. In 1975, the American Psychiatric Association officially dropped homosexuality as a mental disorder. Today's young people grew up with media exposure about homosexuality like no other generation has. Use this TalkSheet to discuss with your kids how Christians and the church can love the homosexual and hate the sin of homosexuality.

To Introduce the Topic:

Write the word *homosexual* in the middle of a chalkboard or on newsprint. Ask the young people to name other words people call homosexuals and write them around the word *homosexual*. Possible words are *gays, fags, queers, fairies, dykes,* and *butch*. Maintain a level of civility and respectability while doing this. When the list appears complete, process the activity by asking the group the following questions.

1. Why do people use such derogatory labels to describe someone?
2. How might someone feel if he or she was called any of these names?

Explain to the group that we label what scares us and what we do not understand. Then tell the group you are going to have a TalkSheet discussion on the issue of homosexuality in order to foster understanding among Christians.

The Discussion:

Item #1: Most young people will know of a homosexual through the mass media.

Item #2: Create a list of fears and then categorize them into two or three fears.

Item #3: The Bible teaches that the homosexual act is a sin, but many young people now see it as an alternative lifestyle no better or worse than other sexual behaviors. As Christians have become more tolerant of sex outside of marriage, they have had to also become more tolerant of homosexual sin. Sin is sin and people know it. To accept heterosexual sin, one must also accept homosexual sin.

Item #4: Take time to discuss those statements that create disagreement within your group.

Item #5: Talk about ways your group members can demonstrate God's grace without being adversely affected by the lifestyle of homosexuals they know.

Item #6: Debate this question to see how open your church is as a redemptive community and how your group could help the church become one.

Item #7: Leviticus 18:22, Leviticus 20:13, Romans 1:27, 28, and 1 Corinthians 6:9 and 10 all focus on the sin of homosexuality. The other passages all deal with God's love for the sinner. Ask the group to determine why it is often difficult for Christians to separate the sin from the sinner with regard to homosexuality.

To Close the Session:

During the teenage years one may have feelings for the same sex even if they are for a fleeting second. This does not indicate the person is a homosexual. There is a mile-wide difference between what we feel and how we act upon those feelings. Some teenagers will experiment with homosexual behaviors. Again, they are not homosexuals. They need God's forgiveness and grace just like teenagers who experiment with heterosexual behaviors. When the Bible mentions the sin of homosexuality, it usually includes this sin in a long list of others. This puts everyone in the same boat, for we all have sinned. Heterosexual sin is just as much a sin as homosexuality.

Then there are those who persist in their homosexuality. Perhaps it is genetically based, the homosexual grew up in a dysfunctional family, or he or she was sexualized at a young age. Whatever the cause, homosexuals need to hear that Christ died for them and that there is a church available to help them with their sin struggle. Homosexuals do not need our name-calling, our discriminatory actions, or our homophobia. What they need is God's grace. The sin of homosexuality is not the unpardonable sin. The Bible clearly teaches that homosexuality is a sin—a shameful and unnatural act. But the Bible also clearly teaches that Christ came to forgive sin and love sinners. We can do no less.

Outside Activity:

Ask the group to create a list of what homosexuals need most from Christians and the church. This list could be presented to the church missions committee, the church board, the pastoral staff, or other appropriate ministry arm of the church. They could then study the issue and report back to the youth group with a possible plan of action.

YOU GOTTA HAVE FAITH

1 If you took a test that showed how much faith you had in Jesus Christ, what grade do you think you would receive? (Circle only one grade.)

A   B   C   D   F

2 If your friends at school graded the test, what grade do you believe they would give you?

A   B   C   D   F

3 **AGREE** or **DISAGREE** with a statement attributed to Mark Twain: "Faith is believing something you know ain't so!"

___ I agree.

___ I disagree.

WHY? _____

_____

_____

4 Check three of the following reasons why you feel many Christian young people do not take their Christian faith seriously.

___ Living the Christian life is not worth it.
___ Christianity may not be true.
___ Christianity does not work in everyday life.
___ The Christian life is too difficult to live.
___ They don't see the importance of God in everyday living.
___ They don't see the fun in Christianity.
___ They are too busy with other things.
___ Christianity does not make much sense.
___ The Christian life is boring.
___ Christianity is too confusing.
___ Christianity is for old people who are about to die.
___ Give your opinion: _____

5 How should your faith change as you get older? _____

_____

_____

6 Read **Hebrews 11** and name three things you learned about faith.

a. _____

b. _____

c. _____

Date Used: _____

Group: _____

YOU GOTTA HAVE FAITH
Topic: Faith

Purpose of this Session:

Even if one is not aware of it, everyone has faith. Some have faith in themselves, some in science, and some in money. Others put their faith in cults or false religions. Take time to talk about what kind of faith your group members have through a TalkSheet discussion.

To Introduce the Topic:

Make the following road signs and tape them up around the room before the group arrives. You will need to make several of each: *Detour, Stop, One Way, Windy Road, No Exit, Yield, School Crossing Zone, Pass with Care, Bump, Keep Right Except to Pass, Downhill, Caution,* and *Construction Ahead.* Ask each person to choose a sign that best represents his or her faith today. Then allow the group members to share what they chose and why. Pass out the TalkSheets and continue the discussion.

The Discussion:

Item #1: Ask the teens if the grades they chose reflect how seriously they live out their faith.

Item #2: Have group members compare the grades they gave themselves with the grades they feel their friends might give them. If there is a discrepancy between the two, ask them why.

Item #3: Ask why many view faith as a crazy belief in something that is not true, but they believe in it anyway. Then talk about what the students are putting their faith into—the church, a set of beliefs found in a book, a quest for the meaning of life, or an historical Jesus who *is* who he says he is.

Item #4: Examine the reasons your kids believe some young people do not take their faith seriously. What distracts teenagers from their faith? Also examine why some young people do take their faith seriously. Is it easier for young people to live with or without faith in Christ? Is the Christian life worth it?

Item #5: Explore how one's faith may change throughout life, especially during the next stage of life, the college-career years. Talk about whether or not the students' faith will be strengthened or weakened by questioning their beliefs and faith. Will it become more or less important?

Item #6: Create a master list of everyone's responses. Take one or two of the Bible characters mentioned in Hebrews 11 and review their relationships to faith.

To Close the Session:

Explain that many people talk about faith in terms of "believing that." They believe that there is a God or that one should go to church. But is "believing that" the kind of faith that God wants? There is nothing wrong with "believing that" faith, which focuses on information. The Bible says even the demons believe (James 2:19). But there is another kind of faith, a "believing in" faith. This kind of faith agrees with God. It is based upon facts like "believing that" faith, but it runs deeper. It is a relational faith that focuses on the person of God and his love. "Believing in" faith is based upon sound historical, factual information. God did not expect us to walk around lost and in the dark. The Bible provides us with the facts of our faith, but we still must have that "believe in" faith to have a personal relationship with Jesus Christ.

Outside Activity:

Tape a large piece of newsprint to the wall and provide marking pens. Ask the young people to write short communications to God about their faith.